CW01501306

Las Vegas Nevada Travel Guide 2023-2024

Sin City Wonders: Your Adventure Starts Here in Las Vegas

Michelle K. Cordell

Table Of Contents

INTRODUCTION

Nestled amid the dry embrace of the Mojave Desert, Las Vegas is a city that calls with its appeal. Let's begin on a trip to discover the soul of this magnificent site.

Long before the glittering lights and lavish casinos, Las Vegas was a modest halt for tired travelers on their way to California. However, the early 1900s represented a turning point. Visionaries started developing hotels and casinos that would transform the city. Over time, Las Vegas grew into the world's leading center of entertainment and excitement.

Picture a city cradled by enormous desert vistas - that's Las Vegas! Nestled in a wide valley, encircled by rocky mountain ranges, this city is a natural treasure. The famed Las Vegas Strip, the focus of action, spans along a boulevard filled with luxurious hotels, beautiful lights, and an unending selection of entertainment.

Las Vegas isn't simply a destination; it's a global crossroads. Here, you'll experience a kaleidoscope of civilizations from throughout the earth. The city is famed for its 'round-the-clock lifestyle, where you can sample world-class food, watch magnificent performances, and engage in adventurous excursions at any hour.

In the pages of this book, I'll dig further into the tapestry of Las Vegas. From the world-famous Strip to hidden gems, from the adrenaline rush of the casinos to the natural marvels that surround the city, Las Vegas is a place of unlimited possibilities. It's a place where aspirations become reality, where the exceptional is within grasp. Together, let's explore this arid oasis and find its various sides.

CHAPTER 1: EXPLORE LAS VEGAS

Exploring Las Vegas is a wonderful journey. From the famed Las Vegas Strip with its brilliant lights and world-class entertainment to the natural marvels of the adjacent Red Rock Canyon, there's something for everyone. Take a walk through famed casinos, enjoy a live concert, or go out to view the Grand Canyon. Las Vegas provides an assortment of gastronomic pleasures and retail opportunities, making it a destination that mixes entertainment, luxury, and natural beauty. Get ready for a spectacular, neon-lit excursion in the Entertainment Capital of the World!

Discover Must-See Places

When touring Las Vegas, there are some must-see locations that you shouldn't miss:

1. Las Vegas Strip: The core of the city, famed for its famous resorts, casinos, and pulsating nightlife. Take a stroll or get on the monorail to visit the many themed hotels including the Bellagio, Caesars Palace, and The Venetian.

2. **Fremont Street Experience:** Located in downtown Las Vegas, it's a pedestrian mall famed for its brilliant light displays and live entertainment. Don't forget to check out the SlotZilla Zip Line for an exciting adventure above the street.

3. **Red Rock Canyon National Conservation Area:** A short drive from the city, this natural marvel provides hiking, rock climbing, and scenic driving among spectacular red sandstone formations.

4. **Hoover Dam:** Just 30 miles from Vegas, this engineering wonder on the Colorado River is worth a visit. Take a tour to learn about its history and development.

5. **The Mob Museum:** Located in Las Vegas, this interactive museum digs into the interesting history of organized crime in America.

6. Neon Boneyard: Discover a collection of antique neon signage from legendary Las Vegas restaurants. Guided tours give insight into the city's history.

7. Springs Preserve: A calm respite in the city, this park contains floral gardens, animal exhibits, and informational displays on desert ecology.

8. High Roller: The world's highest observation wheel, affording amazing views of the city. Enjoy a ride during the day or when the Strip lights up at night.

9. Seven Magic Mountains: A short drive from Las Vegas, this public art piece showcases multicolored piled rocks set against the desert backdrop.

10. Stratosphere Tower: For thrill-seekers, this tower provides exciting rides at extraordinary heights, as well as panoramic views of the city.

These attractions reflect the range of experiences you may have in Las Vegas, from the glitter and glamor of the Strip to the natural beauty of the surrounding desert.

Find Your Way Around

Navigating Las Vegas may be a snap if you know your way around. Here's how to find your way around this bustling city:

1. **The Las Vegas Strip:** The Strip stretches roughly 4 miles along Las Vegas Boulevard South. It's the city's primary artery, and most of the major resorts, casinos, and attractions are situated here.

2. **Monorail:** The Las Vegas Monorail provides a simple method to travel along the Strip. It travels from the MGM Grand in the south to the Sahara Las Vegas (previously the SLS) in the north, with stops at other prominent hotels in between.

3. Deuce and SDX Buses: Operated by the Regional Transportation Commission (RTC), these buses travel 24/7 along the Strip. The Deuce is a double-decker bus, but the SDX (Strip & Downtown Express) is speedier with fewer stops.

4. Taxis and Ride-sharing: Taxis are commonly accessible at hotels and transit hubs. Uber and Lyft also operate in Las Vegas, offering easy trips inside the city.

5. Free Hotel Shuttles: Some hotels provide free shuttle services to popular sites like downtown Las Vegas or outlet malls. Check with your hotel for availability and scheduling.

6. Walking: The Strip is pedestrian-friendly, with well-marked crosswalks and bridges. Exploring on foot is a terrific way to take in the sights, particularly in the nights when the street comes alive with lights and entertainment.

7. Trams: Some resorts feature trams that link them to other properties. For example, the Mandalay Bay–Luxor–Excalibur Tram is a practical method to commute between these three resorts.

8. Renting a Vehicle: If you want to tour locations outside of the city, renting a vehicle might be useful. However, parking costs at most resorts may mount up rapidly.

9. Interactive Maps and Applications: Download maps and navigation applications to your smartphone. Google Maps and Waze operate well in Las Vegas and can help you locate directions and estimated journey times.

10. Tourist Centers: The Las Vegas Convention and Visitors Authority administers various tourist centers throughout the Strip. They give maps, brochures, and valuable information about the city.

11. GPS and Wayfinding Signage: Las Vegas is recognized for its huge, colorful wayfinding signage.

These may be very beneficial for walkers and vehicles alike.

12. Taxi Stands: When departing a resort or attraction, seek marked taxi stands. Avoid taking rides from unauthorized drivers.

By utilizing these transit alternatives and services, you'll be able to travel to Las Vegas with ease and make the most of your vacation.

Hidden Gems Worth Visiting

While Las Vegas is famed for its glamorous casinos and nightlife, it also contains numerous hidden treasures that are well worth seeing. Here are some off-the-beaten-path attractions to discover:

1. Neon Boneyard: Located within the Neon Museum, this outdoor display features retired neon signs from prominent Las Vegas landmarks. It's a distinctive and vivid part of the city's past.

2. The Underground at The Mob Museum: Tucked under The Mob Museum, this speakeasy-style bar provides Prohibition-era beverages in an atmosphere that takes you back to the 1920s.

3. Valley of Fire State Park: Just an hour's drive from the Strip, this park is a natural paradise with spectacular red sandstone formations, petroglyphs, and hiking trails.

4. Seven Magic Mountains: This artwork by Ugo Rondinone displays seven towering piles of vividly colored stones set against the desert environment. It's a startling contrast to the city's glamor.

5. The Arts District: Located just north of downtown, this district is home to galleries, studios, shops, and some of the city's greatest street art. First Fridays feature a thriving arts and cultural scene.

6. Pinball Hall of Fame: For a nostalgic excursion, explore this large pinball and arcade game collection. It's a fun and participatory experience for all ages.

7. Spring Mountain Ranch State Park: Situated in the Red Rock Canyon National Conservation Area, this historic ranch provides guided tours of the former home of billionaire Howard Hughes.

8. The Smith Center for the Performing Arts: A little further from the Strip, this gorgeous facility showcases world-class entertainment, from Broadway productions to concerts by the Las Vegas Philharmonic.

9. Chinatown Plaza: Off the main tourist trail, Las Vegas's Chinatown provides a selection of genuine Asian restaurants and unusual businesses. Don't miss the opportunity to experience this gastronomic gem.

10. The Animal Habitat at the Flamingo: Located directly on the Strip, the Flamingo Hotel's animal habitat is a quiet area to watch Chilean flamingos, swans, turtles, and koi fish among beautiful gardens.

11. Clark County Wetlands Park: A serene respite, this park provides walking pathways and bird-watching possibilities. It's a dramatic contrast to the city's buzz and bustle.

12. Lake Las Vegas: Just a short drive from the Strip, this manmade lake provides water activities, eating, and a quiet retreat from the city's excitement.

Exploring these hidden jewels will offer you a greater appreciation for Las Vegas beyond its iconic casinos, making your experience even more memorable.

Enjoy Lavish Experiences on a Budget

Las Vegas provides a broad choice of opulent experiences that may be experienced even if you're on a budget. Here's how you may indulge in luxury without breaking the bank:

1. Happy Hour Deals: Many posh restaurants and bars in Las Vegas offer happy hour deals with reduced food and beverages. It's a fantastic opportunity to taste gourmet food without the exorbitant price tag.

2. Free Spectacles and Attractions: While the city is renowned for its pricy entertainment, you may see free spectacles like the Bellagio Fountains, Mirage Volcano, or the Fall of Atlantis show at Caesars Palace. Explore the Venetian's Grand Canal Shoppes for a flavor of Venice without spending a dollar.

3. Buffet Eating: Las Vegas is famed for its buffets, and some of them, like the Bacchanal Buffet at Caesars Palace or the Wynn Buffet, provide a gourmet eating experience at moderate costs. Lunch buffets are frequently cheaper than supper.

4. Pool Parties: Enjoy the Vegas pool party scene without the hefty cover charges by coming early or taking advantage of special specials. Pool parties at locations like Encore Beach Club provide a taste of luxurious life.

5. Gaming on a Budget: Set a gaming budget and adhere to it. Look for minimal minimum bets at casino tables or try your luck at penny slots. Many casinos also offer incentives and loyalty programs that might win you free play or discounts.

6. Day Spas: Luxuriate in a spa experience without the luxurious expense. Many hotels include spa facilities that provide cheaply priced treatments, particularly during off-peak hours.

7. Outlet Shopping: Las Vegas offers various outlet malls including Las Vegas North Premium Outlets and Las Vegas South Premium Outlets. You may discover designer brands at cheap prices.

8. Cirque du Soleil Discounts: If you're interested in watching a Cirque du Soleil performance, seek inexpensive tickets via authorized dealers, promotions, or by reserving in advance.

9. Complimentary Beverages: While gaming at casinos, take advantage of free beverages supplied to gamblers. Just remember to tip your server.

10. Hotel Offers: Keep a lookout for hotel offers and packages that include meal credits, spa credits, or play tickets. Booking throughout the week or during the offseason might also result in reduced accommodation costs.

11. Hiking and Nature: Explore the amazing natural splendor around Las Vegas. Red Rock Canyon and Valley of Fire State Park provide hiking and outdoor pleasures at a cheap cost.

12. Uber and Lyft: Using rideshare services may frequently be cheaper than regular taxis, particularly if you're traveling with a group.

By preparing intelligently, taking advantage of specials, and being aware of your spending, you may enjoy the splendor of Las Vegas without emptying your pocketbook.

Take a Dip in the Finest Pools

Las Vegas is famed for its magnificent pools, and here are some of the greatest pool experiences you can enjoy:

1. **Mandalay Bay Beach:** This 11-acre tropical sanctuary contains a large wave pool, lazy river, and a genuine sand beach. It's like a beach vacation in the center of the desert. You may hire cabanas or bungalows for a private and elegant poolside experience.

2. **The Venetian Pool Deck:** The Venetian boasts numerous pools situated in an exquisite Italian-inspired atmosphere. The main pool is a nice spot to relax, and the private cabanas give shade and seclusion. The Tao Beach Club, situated in The Venetian, is a high-energy pool party scene throughout the day.

3. **Caesars Palace Garden of the Gods Pool Oasis:** This amazing complex features seven unique pools, each with its theme and ambiance. You may recline in luxury

or swim in elegance among Roman-inspired buildings and beautiful vegetation.

4. Bellagio Pools: The Bellagio's five pools create a calm and sophisticated ambiance. The Cypress Pool is the most elite, with its Mediterranean-inspired decor and private cabanas. You may also enjoy views of the famed Bellagio Fountains.

5. Encore Beach Club: Known for its exciting day parties, Encore Beach Club provides a busy pool scene with top DJs, a big pool deck, and beautiful cabanas. It's a magnet for people wanting a party environment.

6. The Cosmopolitan's Pool District: This stylish hotel has a series of pools, including the Marquee Dayclub Pool with its vibrant environment, and the Boulevard Pool with its breathtaking views of the Strip. You may even book a separate cabana for extra luxury.

7. Wynn's European Pool: The European-style pool at the Wynn provides a serene and refined setting. It's an adults-only pool where you can take a calm swim or rest in a luxury cabana.

8. **The Mirage Pool:** The Mirage's pool complex has a beautiful tropical environment with waterfalls and a tranquil ambiance. It's a terrific location to relax and enjoy a more laid-back pool experience.

9. **Golden Nugget's The Tank:** This downtown hotel boasts a unique pool with a big shark tank. You may swim alongside these intriguing critters via a transparent acrylic tube. It's an interesting spin on the standard pool experience.

10. **Red Rock Casino Resort & Spa:** If you prefer a calmer pool setting, the Sandbar Pool at Red Rock provides a tranquil refuge with spectacular views of the Red Rock Canyon. Private cabanas are offered for enhanced comfort.

Remember that many of these pools may have entrance prices or access limitations for non-hotel guests, particularly during pool parties and activities. It's a good idea to verify the hotel's regulations and make reservations if you're seeking a certain experience. Whether you're looking for a party scene or a calm escape, Las Vegas offers a pool to fit your interests.

Savor Meals by Renowned Chefs

Las Vegas is a gastronomic wonderland with a myriad of dining choices from world-renowned chefs. Here are some noteworthy places where you may experience dishes by renowned culinary masters:

1. Joël Robuchon at the Mansion: This Michelin three-star restaurant, situated in the MGM Grand, provides an exceptional French dining experience by the late Joël Robuchon. Indulge in a multi-course tasting meal with outstanding foods in an attractive and private atmosphere.

2. Guy Savoy: Found in Caesars Palace, Guy Savoy's restaurant has received three Michelin stars. Enjoy the creativity of this famed French chef with his unique and seasonal recipes, including his famous artichoke and black truffle soup.

3. Restaurant Guy Savoy: Also situated inside Caesars Palace, this is a more informal dining choice by Guy Savoy. It provides a range of distinctive dishes in a less formal ambiance while yet offering great French cuisine.

4. é by José Andrés: Tucked away inside Jaleo at The Cosmopolitan, é is an intimate dining experience like no other. This unique eight-seat restaurant features a tasting menu of avant-garde Spanish tapas crafted by the famous José Andrés.

5. Twist by Pierre Gagnaire: Found in the Waldorf Astoria, Twist features a menu designed by Chef Pierre Gagnaire, a Michelin three-star chef. Enjoy contemporary French cuisine with a twist while taking in panoramic views of the Las Vegas Strip.

6. Gordon Ramsay Hell's Kitchen: Located in Caesars Palace, this restaurant is inspired by the TV program Hell's Kitchen. You may enjoy meals cooked with Gordon Ramsay's unique flare in a vibrant ambiance.

7. Wolfgang Puck's CUT: Situated in The Palazzo, CUT by Wolfgang Puck provides a modern take on the traditional steakhouse. Savor the best cuts of meat in a classy atmosphere.

8. Bobby Flay's Mesa Grill: Visit Caesars Palace to enjoy the delicacies of Bobby Flay, an Iron Chef. His Southwestern-inspired dishes, like his famed blue corn pancake, are a must-try.

9. Le Cirque: Located in Bellagio, this famous French restaurant provides a spectacular dining experience. It's a culinary jewel where you can taste perfectly prepared cuisine in a refined atmosphere.

10. Mizumi: Situated at Wynn Las Vegas, Mizumi delivers Japanese cuisine with flare. Enjoy sushi, robatayaki, and teppanyaki in a magnificent location overlooking a quiet Japanese garden.

11. Carnevino by Mario Batali and Joe Bastianich: At The Palazzo, Carnevino is a steakhouse by renowned chefs Mario Batali and Joe Bastianich. It's noted for its outstanding steaks and Italian-inspired cuisine.

These are just a handful of the many excellent restaurants

Get Ready with Entertainment Recommendations

With regards to diversion, Las Vegas doesn't frustrate. Here are some entertainment tips to guarantee you have a great time in the city:

1. World-Class Shows
- **Cirque du Soleil:** Las Vegas is home to various Cirque du Soleil shows, including "O" at Bellagio, "Michael Jackson ONE" at Mandalay

Bay, and "The Beatles LOVE" at The Mirage. These captivating displays blend acrobatics, music, and breathtaking images.

- **Magic Shows:** Enjoy mind-bending magic acts by famous magicians like David Copperfield at the MGM Grand and Criss Angel at Planet Hollywood.
- **Comedy Clubs:** Catch stand-up comedy performers at locations like The Comedy Cellar at Rio All-Suite Hotel and Casino or Brad Garrett's Comedy Club at MGM Grand.

2. Concerts & Music Events

- Check the schedules of major arenas and musical venues including T-Mobile Arena, MGM Grand Garden Arena, and The Colosseum at Caesars Palace. Top performers regularly perform here.
- For live music and DJ performances, visit nightlife destinations including XS at Encore, Marquee at The Cosmopolitan, and Omnia at Caesars Palace.

3. Nightlife

- Experience the bustling nightlife of Las Vegas at legendary nightclubs including XS, Marquee, Omnia, and Drai's Beachclub & Nightclub.
- Enjoy rooftop bars with spectacular views, such as The Chandelier at The Cosmopolitan and VooDoo Rooftop Nightclub at Rio All-Suite Hotel and Casino.

4. Casino Gaming

- Try your luck at the city's world-famous casinos, including Bellagio, Caesars Palace, The Venetian, and Wynn Las Vegas. Whether you're a seasoned gambler or a newbie, there's something for everyone.

5. Outdoor Entertainment

- Watch the stunning Fountains of Bellagio, a free outdoor water display synchronized to music and lighting.

- Explore the Fremont Street Experience in downtown Las Vegas, noted for its LED canopy and nightly light displays.

6. Theater Productions

- Enjoy Broadway-style shows and musicals at places like The Smith Center for the Performing Arts.
- Look for traveling shows and resident acts at different resort theaters.

7. Sports Event

- Depending on the season, see NHL hockey with the Vegas Golden Knights at T-Mobile Arena or NFL football with the Las Vegas Raiders at Allegiant Stadium.

8. Adult Entertainment

- Las Vegas provides adult-themed performances like "Absinthe" at Caesars Palace and "Zumanity" by Cirque du Soleil at New York-New York.

9. Escape Rooms and Interactive Experiences

- Challenge your brains and problem-solving abilities at escape rooms like The Basement: A Live Escape Room Experience.
- Try unique activities such as the Virtual Reality Escape Room at Level Up at MGM Grand.

10. Dinner and a Show

- Many restaurants offer dinner-and-show packages, combining a gourmet dining experience with live entertainment.

11. Off-Broadway Productions

- Explore smaller venues for unusual and eccentric performances that appeal to varied interests.

Before your travel, verify the dates and availability of these entertainment alternatives and consider reserving tickets in advance, particularly for popular performances and events. Las Vegas offers plenty to offer every tourist, from magnificent spectacles to intimate shows, assuring you'll find entertainment that meets your interests.

Discover Fun Activities That Don't Cost a Thing

Exploring Las Vegas on a budget is not only doable but also entertaining. Here are some free or low-cost activities that can add enjoyment to your visit:

1. **Bellagio Fountains:** Witness the amazing Bellagio Fountains. These water-choreographed performances synchronized to music and lights take place often in the evenings and are a pleasure to see.

2. **The Volcano at The Mirage:** The Mirage presents a volcanic explosion spectacle with fire, smoke, and lava spewing from a man-made volcano. It's a riveting experience, and it's free.

3. **The Wildlife Habitat at Flamingo:** Visit the Wildlife Habitat at the Flamingo Hotel, home to Chilean flamingos, swans, ducks, and koi fish. It's like a peaceful haven on the Strip.

4. The LINQ Promenade: Stroll along The LINQ Promenade, an open-air retail and eating center. It's a terrific area for people-watching and regularly features free live entertainment.

5. Fremont Street Experience: Head to downtown Las Vegas and experience the Fremont Street Experience. It has a giant LED canopy with light displays and live music acts.

6. Red Rock Canyon National Conservation Area: While located in the city core, Red Rock Canyon provides spectacular desert scenery. There's a minimal admission charge per car, making it a cheap day excursion for wildlife enthusiasts.

7. Seven Magic Mountains: Visit the Seven Magic Mountains, a beautiful art piece in the desert approximately 10 miles south of Las Vegas. It's a unique picture opportunity.

8. Arts District: Explore the Las Vegas Arts District. It's recognized for its bright street art, galleries, and unique stores. First Friday, a monthly arts and cultural celebration, is worth visiting.

9. Container Park: The Container Park in downtown Las Vegas contains boutique stores, restaurants, and a playground. It's created completely from shipping containers.

10. Conservatory & Botanical Gardens at Bellagio: The Bellagio Conservatory & Botanical Gardens regularly offer seasonal exhibits and magnificent flower arrangements. It's free to enter.

11. Wildlife Habitat at Springs Preserve: Hot Springs Preserve provides a natural habitat where visitors may encounter native creatures, like desert tortoises, and learn about the local environment.

12. Sunset Park: Enjoy a day at Sunset Park, a neighborhood favorite with picnic spaces, playgrounds, and walking paths.

13. Pinball Hall of Fame: Visit the Pinball Hall of Fame, where you may play antique pinball machines and classic arcade games. It's a unique and nostalgic experience.

14. Hoover Dam Bypass Bridge: Take a short trip to the Hoover Dam Bypass Bridge. The vistas of the Hoover Dam and Colorado River are breathtaking, and there's no fee to visit.

15. Ethel M Chocolate Factory: Tour the Ethel M Chocolate Factory, where you can watch the chocolate-making process and try some tasty delicacies.

These activities provide a combination of entertainment, environment, and culture without breaking the wallet. Las Vegas has lots to offer beyond the casinos and entertainment, making it a perfect destination for budget-conscious vacationers.

Plan Your Dream Las Vegas Wedding

Planning a perfect Las Vegas wedding may be an exciting and memorable experience. Here's a step-by-step guide to help you make it a reality:

1. Choose the Date and Venue: Select a date that works for you and your spouse. Las Vegas provides a range of sites, from beautiful chapels to gorgeous outdoor locales. Some popular settings are the Little White Wedding Chapel, Graceland Wedding Chapel, and Red Rock Canyon.

2. Obtain a Marriage License: Before getting married in Las Vegas, you'll need to get a marriage license from the Clark County Marriage Bureau. Both you and your companion must be present and produce acceptable identification. There's a charge for the license, and there's no waiting time.

3. Find the Perfect Officiant: Choose an officiant who can execute your ceremony. Many wedding chapels in Las Vegas provide officiants as part of their packages. You may also engage an independent officiant if you like a certain wedding style.

4. Customize Your Ceremony: Work with your officiant to tailor your wedding ceremony. Whether you choose a conventional, themed, or customized wedding, Las Vegas can meet your desires.

5. Plan the Reception: Decide whether you want a modest intimate reception or a huge extravaganza. Las Vegas offers various restaurants, hotels, and banquet facilities that can host your reception. Consider if you want a sit-down meal, buffet, or something more distinctive.

6. Book Photography and Videography: Capture every detail of your big day by hiring a professional photographer and filmmaker. They may help you build memorable memories.

7. Arrange Transportation: If you're going to numerous sites for your wedding and reception, coordinate transportation for you and your guests. Limousines and party buses are popular alternatives.

8. Get Your Wedding Attire: Find the appropriate wedding clothing for both the bride and groom. Las Vegas features bridal shops, tuxedo rental establishments, and boutiques where you may shop for your wedding outfit.

9. Plan Entertainment: Consider entertainment choices for your reception, such as a DJ, live band, or even a celebrity impersonation. Las Vegas offers a vast selection of talent to pick from.

10. Handle Legal Details: Ensure all legal issues are taken care of, including submitting your marriage license after the ceremony. Your officiant or chapel personnel may aid with this.

11. Invitations & Guest List: If you're inviting visitors, generate invites and manage your guest list. Las Vegas wedding chapels typically sell packages that include invitations and other items.

12. Decor & Flowers: Choose your wedding décor and flower arrangements. Whether you want something basic or complex, there are lots of alternatives in Las Vegas.

13. Wedding Rings: Select your wedding bands, which are symbolic of your commitment to each other. Las Vegas features jewelry boutiques where you may discover unique and classic designs.

14. Marriage Certificate: After your wedding, be sure to secure numerous copies of your marriage certificate. You may need them for legal considerations or if you wish to alter your last name.

15. Enjoy Your Special Day: On your wedding day, relax, absorb the moment, and enjoy your fantasy Las

Vegas wedding. Cherish the memories you're building in this dynamic and interesting city.

Remember that Las Vegas provides a broad choice of wedding alternatives to suit diverse preferences and budgets, making it a popular location for couples wishing to tie the knot uniquely and memorably.

CHAPTER 2: TRAVELING WISELY

Making wise decisions and preparation are essential to a comfortable and happy trip.

Important Advice for Your Trip

Careful preparation is necessary while getting ready for a vacation to guarantee a comfortable and pleasurable experience. Here are some crucial pointers to help you maximize your vacation experience:

1. Do Some Research Before You Go: Do an extensive study on your location before you go. Discover its history, traditions, legislation, and main tourist destinations. Having a basic understanding of the culture might improve your vacation experience.

2. Organize a Schedule: Create a flexible schedule that incorporates the must-see sights and activities but leaves room for improvisation. This keeps space for exploring while ensuring you don't miss the must-see attractions.

3. Verify Your Passport and Visa Requirements: Check that your passport is valid for at least six months after the date of your return. Check the destination's visa requirements and apply early if required.

4. Travel Light: Choose adaptable attire and just bring what you need when you pack. Think about the weather where you're going and prepare appropriately.

5. Travel Protection: Invest in travel insurance to safeguard yourself against unforeseen occurrences like trip cancellations, medical problems, or misplaced baggage.

6. Protect Critical Documents: Make copies of your passport, identification, trip itinerary, and crucial contact details. Keep these copies apart from your original documents.

7. Money Issues: To prevent card problems, let your bank know about your vacation intentions. Bring a variety of payment options with you, such as cash, credit cards, and a backup method.

8. Maintain Contact: Make sure your phone is functional overseas. If you want to communicate cheaply, think about purchasing local SIM cards or international roaming packages.

9. Warnings for Your Health: Visit your doctor for any immunizations or prescriptions that are necessary. A basic first-aid kit and any required prescription drugs should be carried.

10. Basics of Language: Acquire a few basic words and expressions in the native tongue, such as salutations and polite expressions. The people there admire your attempt to speak their language.

11. Pack Wisely: Utilize packing cubes or organizers to keep your possessions accessible and arranged. Don't forget the necessities, like toiletries, adapters, and chargers.

12. Apps for Travel: Download navigation, language translation, money conversion, and local advice applications before your trip. Offline maps may be quite helpful.

13. Safety Measures: Pay attention to your surroundings, particularly in strange places. Use hotel safes, keep your possessions safe, and steer clear of nighttime solo wandering.

14. Responsible Environmental Behavior: Travel sustainably by minimizing waste, preserving resources, and assisting projects that promote sustainable tourism.

15. Adopt a Local Perspective: Get involved with the community by sampling local cuisine, going to cultural events, and mingling with the populace. Observe regional traditions and customs.

16. Stay Up to Date: Pay attention to local news and warnings, particularly if you're visiting places where there may be security issues.

17. Lightweight Travel: Take into account how your trips may affect the environment. Use reusable materials, reduce waste, and encourage companies to operate sustainably.

18. Unwind and Enjoy: Keep in mind that traveling is an experience, and things sometimes may not go as expected. Take in every moment, embrace the adventure, and be receptive to new experiences.

You may improve your vacation, remain secure, and make lasting memories in your selected location by adhering to this vital travel advice.

City Navigation

It may be both exhilarating and difficult to get to a new city. Here are some thorough pointers to make it easier for you to move about a city:

1. Pick up a City Map: Request a city map from your lodging or a tourist information center. Learn the key thoroughfares, landmarks, and locations of public transit.

2. Utilize Navigational Apps and GPS: Download a city-specific app or navigation software like Google Maps to assist you in navigating your way around. In case your mobile service is lost, download maps to your computer.

3. Using Public Transit: Learn about the city's transit options, such as buses, trams, subways, and commuter trains. For easy transportation, buy tickets or passes.

4. Walkability: When feasible, explore the city on foot. You may uncover hidden jewels and get fully immersed in the community by walking.

5. Services for Sharing Rides: If you want quick, on-demand transportation, think about utilizing a ride-sharing service like Uber or Lyft. Verify the driver's identification and the particulars of the automobile to make sure you're safe.

6. Taxis: Only use authorized taxi services, and ensure that the meter is on. In the event of a communication breakdown, carry the address of your destination with you in the local tongue.

7. Scooters and Bicycles: Programs for sharing bikes and scooters are available in several places. Renting a bike or scooter is an effective and environmentally responsible way to move about.

8. Cards for Local Transportation: Find out whether the city provides transportation cards that allow unrestricted use of public transportation for a certain period. These may result in fare savings.

9. A City Tour: Take one of the many narrated city tours or hop-on, hop-off bus excursions to learn about the city's highlights. These excursions often include historical context and discussion.

10. Roadside Symbols and Landmarks: To assist you in getting around, pay attention to street signs, landmarks, and prominent structures. Major attractions are marked with signage in many cities.

11. Query Locals: Don't be shy about seeking advice from locals or asking for directions. Most folks are eager to assist travelers and may provide insightful information.

12. Considerations for Safety: Be mindful of your surroundings, particularly in busy or strange places. To avoid theft, safeguard your possessions.

13. Make a Plan: Schedule your daily trips in advance, particularly if you have many locations. This may lessen your stress and help you make the most of your time.

14. Discover Basic Phrases: Learn the keywords and expressions for greetings, asking for directions, and asking typical inquiries in the language of the area.

15. Apps for Local Transportation: Official transportation applications in certain places provide up-to-the-minute information on routes, delays, and timetables. These applications may be really helpful.

16. Numerals for Emergencies: Save police, ambulance, and diplomatic contacts as well as other local emergency numbers on your phone.

17. Maintain Contact: Check the battery life on your smartphone and think about keeping a portable charger or power bank with you for unexpected situations.

18. Just Wait: Getting about in a new city might be difficult at times. Keep calm and don't let momentary setbacks or erroneous turns demotivate you.

With these pointers in hand, you may explore a new city with confidence, learn about its attractions, and maximize your trip experience.

Travel Essentials

It is essential for a seamless and pleasurable vacation that you have all the necessary travel information at your fingertips. The following are the essential travel preparations to make:

1. Permits and Passports: Verify that your passport is valid for at least six months after the dates of your trip. Check the destination's visa requirements and apply for one if necessary.

2. Travel Protection: Invest in comprehensive travel insurance that includes coverage for lost luggage, trip cancellation, and medical emergencies. Keep a copy of the specifics of your policy.

3. Flight Schedule: Have a copy of your flight itinerary, including the time of departure and arrival, the contact details for the airline, and the booking reference, printed or stored electronically.

4. Information on Lodging: Keep track of the addresses, phone numbers, and confirmation numbers for any hotel or vacation rental arrangements you make.

5. Emergency Numbers: Save crucial phone numbers, such as those for your country's embassy or consulate and the emergency services in your area, on your phone.

6. Currency Details: Acquaint yourself with the banking options, exchange rates, and local currency at your location. To prevent card problems, inform your bank of your trip dates.

7. Travel Papers: Arrange all trip-related papers in a safe folder or digital wallet, including tickets, boarding cards, and travel vouchers.

8. Record of Vaccinations: If necessary, bring proof of immunization and medical documents. Do plenty of prior research on any vaccinations required for your travel.

9. Transport Information: Keep maps of public transit, bookings for auto rentals, and train or bus timetables close at hand.

10. Schedule and Maps: Make a thorough vacation itinerary that includes daily schedules, attraction locations, and dinner reservations. Save destination maps to your computer.

11. Apps for Travel: Download navigation, language translation, currency conversion, and local suggestions applications to aid with your travels.

12. Resources for Language: Keep a phrasebook or language-learning app with you for simple local language conversation. Become familiar with frequent expressions.

13. Chargers and Travel Adapters: Be sure to bring the correct power adapters and charges for all of your electronic equipment, such as computers, cameras, and cell phones.

14. Prescription Drugs and Medications: If you regularly take prescription medicine, make sure you have enough for the trip. Bring copies of prescriptions and a list of your medications.

15. Vacation Wallet: Keep cash, cards, and other valuables organized and protected in a travel wallet or bag.

16. First Aid Kit: Assemble a compact emergency kit with goods like personal care items, painkillers, and first aid supplies.

17. Nearby Contacts: Have the phone numbers of any friends or acquaintances you may have who may be able to help you or suggest places to go at your location.

18. Restrictions on Travel: Find out whether your government has issued any cautions or restrictions on travel to your location.

19. Extra Copies: Make copies of or digital scans of important papers, including your passport, visa, and travel insurance policy. Keep them apart from the originals while storing them.

20. Weather and Time Zone: Consider the variation in time zones between your house and your destination. For packing considerations, check the weather forecast for your area.

You'll be more prepared for your travels and more equipped to handle unforeseen circumstances while still fully enjoying your experience if you have these travel-related elements sorted.

Useful People

During your vacation, having a list of helpful contacts might be helpful. The following list of crucial people to take with you when traveling:

1. Services for Emergencies: Before arriving at your location, be aware of the local emergency numbers for the police, ambulance, and fire departments. The emergency number in the majority of European nations is 112.

2. Consulate or Embassy of Your Country: Locate your home country's embassy or consulate in case you run into legal challenges, passport concerns, or other situations.

3. Provider of Travel Insurance: Always have your travel insurance company's contact information handy, including a 24-hour emergency support number. If necessary, be ready to offer specifics about your policy.

4. Local Medical Center or Clinic: Locate the medical facilities that are the closest to your lodging. Keep their contact information close to hand in case you need it for non-emergency medical issues.

5. Neighborhood Police Station: Make a note of the location and phone number of the neighborhood police station. For reporting small occurrences or misplaced objects, this might be useful.

6. Travel Agencies and Airlines: Save the phone numbers and addresses of the hotels, vehicle rental companies, and other travel service providers you use. This is essential for service problems or modifications to the itinerary.

7. Banks and Credit Card Companies: Keep the customer care numbers for your banks and credit card issuers handy. Notify them as soon as possible if your cards are lost or stolen.

8. Friends or Family Members: Tell friends or family about your plan and have their phone numbers handy. They may help if you need local guidance or in an emergency.

9. Travel Agent or Tour Guide: If you're on a guided trip, save the contact information for your tour operator or guide. They may assist with queries and logistics.

10. Providers of Local Transportation: Save the phone numbers for any public transit hotlines, ridesharing applications, or taxi services in your area.

11. Services for Language Assistance: Carry the contact information for language support agencies or interpreters, if available, if you are not proficient in the local tongue.

12. Services for Consuls: For foreign tourists, write down the phone number for the closest consulate office in your nation. They can help with a variety of overseas problems.

13. Services for the Lost and Found: Recognize how to reach out to local lost and found agencies if you lose property.

14. Agency for Travel or Tour Operator: If you used a travel agency to arrange your trip, have their contact details on hand in case any concerns or problems should occur.

15. Local Travel Information Office: Discover the location and phone number of the neighborhood tourist information office. They may provide directions, manuals, and useful advice.

16. Lost and Found at Airlines: Know how to contact the airline's lost and found offices if your baggage disappears.

17. Services for Roadside Assistance: If you're driving, know how to reach the emergency number of your vehicle rental business or roadside help services.

18. Wireless Service Provider: Save your mobile network provider's customer support number. Check the data roaming choices and overseas coverage of your phone plan.

19. Reliable Local Contacts: Save the contact information of any friends, acquaintances, or coworkers you may have in the region. They can help and provide local knowledge.

20. Local Tourism Organizations: Save the phone numbers and addresses of any tourist centers or local tourism bureaus. On services and attractions, they may provide advice.

You may travel with more assurance if you have these contacts at your fingertips on your phone or a paper travel document.

CHAPTER 3: EXPLORING NEW LOCATIONS

An excellent approach to discovering a city's distinctive culture and environment is to explore its many neighborhoods. Here's how to research various locations:

1. Study and Plan: Start by doing some research on the city's neighborhoods. Find all about their past, enticing features, and history.

2. Select Your Sectors: Determine the areas in which your interests are shared. Are you interested in historical landmarks, restaurants, shops, or the arts and culture? Choose neighborhoods that suit your tastes.

3. Local Perspectives: Speak with locals or look for advice in forums online. Locals often know undiscovered treasures and may recommend interesting places to visit.

4. Using Public Transit: Get acquainted with the city's public transportation network. Commuter trains, buses, trams, and the underground system all make connecting areas easy.

5. Pedestrian Tours: Take into account signing up for escorted neighborhood walking tours. These trips often include local knowledge and historical background.

6. Food Escapades: Examine several regions' culinary scenes. Every community could have its own peculiarities and distinctive culinary experiences.

7. Cultural Encounters: Look for cultural gatherings, museums, or galleries in various areas. There could be creative and artistic hotspots in certain places.

8. Regional Markets: Go to regional, flea, or farmer's markets. They are great locations to get a taste of the local way of life and discover one-of-a-kind gifts.

9. Unwind and Watch: Sometimes just roaming the streets, witnessing everyday life, and mingling with residents is the greatest way to learn about an area.

10. Safety Measures: Be mindful of your surroundings and follow common safety measures when exploring, such as securing your possessions and avoiding dimly lit places at night.

11. Keep Memories: Take pictures and record your recollections of the many places you visit. These images may serve as wonderful keepsakes and travel memories.

12. Get Out of the Tourist Spots: While it's important to visit well-known tourist destinations, explore less popular locations as well. They often provide more genuine experiences.

13. Keep an Open Mind: Even if the local way of life differs from your own, embrace it. Meaningful encounters might result from interacting with locals and respecting their culture.

It might be pleasant to explore several areas to fully appreciate a city's diversity and develop lifelong trip experiences.

Take a South Strip Tour

In Las Vegas, exploring the South Strip will introduce you to a bustling and varied selection of attractions, restaurants, and entertainment. The following advice will help you get the most out of your trip to this dynamic area of the city:

1. **Beginning at Mandalay Bay:** Start your tour in Mandalay Bay, an opulent resort renowned for its Shark Reef Aquarium and tropical-themed pool area. Swim leisurely or explore the wonderful undersea world.

2. **The Sphinx and Luxor:** The renowned Luxor Hotel, fashioned like a pyramid and including a miniature Sphinx, lies next to Mandalay Bay. If you're interested in history, examine its distinctive architecture and go to the Titanic: The Artifact Exhibition.

3. Hideaway in The Park: Travel north to The Park, a neighborhood with outdoor restaurants and entertainment located between the Park MGM and New York-New York resorts. Take a stroll amid beautiful vegetation while eating outside.

4. Eataly: Eataly at Park MGM, an Italian marketplace with a fantastic range of gourmet goods, eateries, and cafés, is a must-visit if you're a foodie.

5. The City of New York: Take in the atmosphere of New York-New York, the Big Apple. Enjoy New York-style pizza, ride the roller coaster, and see the ornate façade that features NYC landmarks.

6. T-Mobile Arena: View the T-Mobile Arena event calendar. It holds performances, games, and athletic activities. If your visit coincides with an event, attend a game or concert.

7. Park Theater: World-class performances are held nearby at Park MGM's Park Theater during residencies.

Look for forthcoming concerts by well-known performers.

8. A Culinary Adventure: The South Strip offers a variety of eating establishments. For a more premium eating experience, go to Bavette's Steakhouse & Bar or Tom's Urban for comfort cuisine.

9. The Crystals Shops: The Shops at Crystals is the place to go for luxury shopping. High-end stores and premium brands may be found in this mall.

10. Resort & Casino ARIA: Visit the ARIA Resort & Casino, renowned for its cutting-edge architecture and stunning collection of fine art. Additionally, establishments like Julian Serrano Tapas provide exquisite cuisine.

11. The Bellagio Fountains: End your South Strip journey by taking in the spellbinding Bellagio Fountains. These musically orchestrated water shows are a staple of Las Vegas.

12. The Night Emerges: The South Strip comes alive with a thriving entertainment scene as dusk strikes. Drinks may be had at establishments like The Chandelier at The Cosmopolitan or Marquee Nightclub, respectively.

13. Transportation and Safety: Keep in mind to remain hydrated, particularly in the hot desert. While the South Strip is a walking area, lengthier trips may be more appropriate for trams or ridesharing.

A combination of food, entertainment, and culture can be found on the South Strip, which embodies Las Vegas. This vibrant area of the city has plenty to offer everyone, whether they like culture, cuisine, or thrills.

Take a Walk Along the Central Strip

The Central Strip in Las Vegas is a thrilling place to stroll since it is home to famous monuments, brilliant lights, and top-notch entertainment. Here is some advice to make the most of your stroll along this energetic stretch:

1. The Greeting Sign: Commence your trip at the well-known "Welcome to Fabulous Las Vegas" sign. For that famous picture opportunity, it's a must-see.

2. Promenade at The LINQ: Travel to The LINQ Promenade in the north, an outdoor entertainment complex with shops, eateries, and attractions. The High Roller, the tallest observation wheel in the world, offers breathtaking views that shouldn't be missed.

3. A Flamingo: Next, take a tour of The Flamingo, one of Las Vegas's first hotels. See flamingos, ducks, and other exotic birds at the Wildlife Habitat.

4. Caesars Palace's Forum Shops: Continue to The Forum Shops at Caesars Palace, a posh shopping area with a setting influenced by ancient Rome. Discover upscale shops, enjoy fine dining, and be amazed by the "Fall of Atlantis" show.

5. This Mirage: The Mirage across the street hosts an evening show with an erupting volcano. Visit the dolphin habitat and Siegfried & Roy's Secret Garden within.

6. The Palazzo and The Venetian: Travel to The Venetian and The Palazzo in the north to enjoy a gondola ride along the Grand Canal and take in the magnificent architecture. Very good quality shopping can be found at The Shoppes at The Palazzo.

7. Grand Canal Shoppes: Continue to The Grand Canal Shoppes, a mall with a Venice motif, and take in the lovely waterways' window shopping opportunities.

8. TI: Treasure Island: Take a stroll to Treasure Island (TI), where you may take in the outdoor display "Sirens of TI" at no cost. On the open seas, it's a swashbuckling spectacle.

9. Fashion Show Mall: The Fashion Show Mall, a sizable shopping center with a variety of retail establishments, is located across from TI.

10. Las Vegas' Wynn and Encore: Explore the beautiful architecture, landscaped gardens, and works of art at the nearby Wynn Las Vegas and Encore resorts. Don't miss the Wynn's Lake of Dreams performance.

11. The Palazzo's Enchanted Carousel: Check out The Palazzo's charming carousel, which was inspired by Carnevale.

12. The Magnificent Mirage Volcano: Come back to The Mirage in the evening to see the Mirage Volcano's magnificent eruption, which will be accompanied by music and fire displays.

13. The High Roller at The LINQ: To round up your Central Strip exploration, take a ride on the High Roller for sweeping views of the city of Las Vegas at night.

14. Security and Amusement: Always follow crosswalks and pedestrian bridges to keep safe. Enjoy the exciting atmosphere as you take in the street performers, live music, and entertainment that fill the Central Strip.

Walking through the Central Strip gives a captivating tour of the city's core, complete with a fusion of attractions, shopping, and architectural marvels. Whether you're a shopper, a cultural buff, or just seeking an exceptional experience, the Central Strip offers it everything.

Uncover the Charms of the North Strip

Exploring the North Strip in Las Vegas is an amazing excursion loaded with renowned sites, good restaurants, and entertainment. Here's a full guide to help you make the most of your visit to this bustling section of the city:

1. The Stratosphere Tower: Start your experience with the Stratosphere Tower, the highest freestanding observation tower in the United States. Enjoy amazing views of the city from its observation decks.

2. The Neon Graveyard: Discover the Neon Boneyard, a fascinating outdoor museum featuring decommissioned neon signs from prominent Las Vegas landmarks, just north of the Stratosphere.

3. Las Vegas' SLS Hotel: Check out the SLS Las Vegas, a chic resort renowned for its cutting-edge architecture, hip clubs, and José Andrés' Bazaar Meat restaurant.

4. Golf at The Wynn: Visit the Wynn Golf Club, an 18-hole championship golf course situated in a lush, gorgeous setting, which is close to the SLS.

5. The Las Vegas Festival Grounds: Keep heading north until you reach the Las Vegas Festival Grounds, a venue for special events, concerts, and festivals.

6. Cirque du Soleil: Visit Circus Circus, a family-friendly resort with a renowned Adventuredome, an indoor amusement park, and circus shows.

7. Las Vegas's The Drew (Coming Soon): Take a tour of The Drew Las Vegas' future location, a resort and casino that will include opulent lodging and entertainment.

8. The Fireside Lounge at The Peppermill: Visit the Peppermill Fireside Lounge, a legendary Vegas venue famed for it vintage vibe, neon lighting, and distinctive fire pit.

9. The Las Vegas Fashion Outlets: The Fashion Outlets of Las Vegas, which offer discounts on designer products, are a great place for shoppers.

10. International Trade Center: Explore the World Market Center, a center for the furniture and home décor sector that often hosts events and trade exhibits.

11. District of the Arts: Visit the Arts District, which is located south of the Stratosphere, where you can discover galleries, shops, and original art installations.

12. Casino at Main Street Station: The Main Street Station Casino, renowned for its collection of antiques and relics, offers a flavor of history.

13. Mob Museum: The Mob Museum, an interactive exhibit focused on organized crime in Las Vegas, provides information on the history of the mob in the city.

14. Dining: There are several eating alternatives on The North Strip, ranging from fast food joints to fine dining establishments. Make sure you try some of the greatest food the city has to offer.

15. Transportation: There are plenty of buses and ride-sharing options for getting about the North Strip.

16. Nightlife: Enjoy the nighttime scene in the many pubs, clubs, and lounges that feature DJs, live music, and other entertainment.

You may find a combination of contemporary entertainment alternatives and vintage Vegas charm by exploring the North Strip. This region offers both family-friendly and exciting nightlife options, so there is something for everyone.

Explore Las Vegas' Downtown Area

The Fremont Street Experience, or Downtown Las Vegas, is a bustling and interesting area of the city that provides a fascinating counterpoint to the well-known Las Vegas Strip. Here is a thorough guide to help you experience Downtown Las Vegas's energy:

1. Experience with Fremont Street: The Fremont Street Experience, a pedestrian mall renowned for its spectacular light canopy and nightly light displays, is a great place to start your tour. Discover the lively street with its live music, street performers, and festive ambiance.

2. Zipline by SlotZilla: Fly above Fremont Street on the SlotZilla Zip Line to get your heart racing. You have the option of either a lesser zip line or a higher, riskier one.

3. Art Installations and Neon Signs: There are a lot of old neon signs and artworks throughout downtown. Don't forget to see the colorful Container Park, the neon museum, and the famous "Welcome to Fabulous Las Vegas" sign.

4. Casinos on Fremont Street: Try your luck at one of Fremont Street's venerable casinos, such as the Golden Nugget, Four Queens, or Binion. Play games, watch live shows, and eat delicious food.

5. Mob Museum: Take a tour of the Mob Museum, a fascinating attraction devoted to the background of organized crime in Las Vegas and the US. Find out about the notorious mobsters that governed the city in the past.

6. Container Park in the City: Go to the Downtown Container Park, a distinctive eating and retail district constructed from shipping containers. It has upscale stores, dining options, and a children's playground.

7. Creative District: Take a stroll around the adjacent Arts District, home to many studios, galleries, and street art installations. It's a fantastic location to learn about regional art and culture.

8. Nightlife and Dining: There are many different places to eat in Downtown Las Vegas, including fine dining establishments and traditional diners. Enjoy the exciting nightlife that includes live music venues, pubs, and clubs.

9. Performers on the Street: Take in the diverse array of street performers along Fremont Street, including musicians, magicians, and other acts.

10. History of Fremont Street: Check out the historical plaques and exhibits that chronicle the development of Downtown Las Vegas and Fremont Street to learn more about their past.

11. Playground in Container Park: The Container Park Playground is an excellent place for youngsters to burn off some energy if you're traveling with kids.

12. Transportation: Transit options to Downtown Las Vegas include public transit, ride-sharing services, and automobiles. Generally speaking, parking is less expensive than on the Strip.

Downtown Las Vegas is a must-visit location while you're in the city since it has a vibrant and upbeat environment. This region has everything you might want, whether you're looking for fun, history, or a distinctive cultural experience.

Explore Paradise Road's East Side.

Discovering Las Vegas' East Side via Paradise Road offers another viewpoint to the glamor of the Strip. Here is a thorough guide to assist you in finding the local landmarks and tourist attractions:

1. The Convention Center in Las Vegas: Begin your adventure in the biggest conference facility in the world, the Las Vegas conference facility. Check to see if any shows or activities are going on when you are there.

2. Westgate Resort & Casino in Las Vegas: The Westgate Las Vegas Resort & Casino, previously the Las Vegas Hilton, is located just south of the Convention Center. This renowned hotel has eating, gambling, and entertainment choices in addition to a long history.

3. A Barrymore: The Barrymore at the Royal Resort offers a traditional steakhouse experience with a vintage Vegas ambiance. It is renowned for its delicious steaks and drinks.

4. Las Vegas SLS: The SLS Las Vegas, a hip hotel and casino with a variety of culinary choices, including Bazaar Meat by José Andrés, can be found farther south on Paradise Road.

5. The Skypod, Casino, and Hotel at Strata: The Strat Hotel, Casino & Skypod (previously the Stratosphere) is located to the north. This famous tower provides exhilarating rides, a rotating restaurant, and breathtaking cityscape views.

6. Arts District and Arts Factory: Visit the Arts Factory and the nearby Arts District, which are somewhat to the east. The city's artistic aspect is shown via galleries, shops, and art installations.

7. The Museum of Neon: At The Neon Museum, learn about the history of Las Vegas via its famous neon signs. Guided tours provide information on the history of the city's neon.

8. Port Container: The Downtown Container Park, an outdoor retail and entertainment complex with distinctive shops and a playground for children, is just a short drive from Paradise Road.

9. Encore Resorts and Wynn: The opulent Wynn and Encore Resorts are located at the southern end of Paradise Road. Discover their posh eateries, boutiques, and the beautiful Lake of Dreams.

10. Las Vegas Sahara: Sahara Las Vegas provides food, entertainment, and gambling opportunities within a short distance from Paradise Road.

11. Country Club of Las Vegas: If you like playing golf, you may want to visit the storied Las Vegas Country Club, which is close to Paradise Road.

12. Access via Monorail: Paradise Road offers simple access to the Las Vegas Monorail, which links the Convention Center and several significant resorts to the Strip.

13. Transportation: Paradise Road is easily reached by automobile, ride-hailing services, and public transit. In most cases, parking is offered at attractions.

From eating and gambling to art and culture, the East Side of Las Vegas, centered on Paradise Road, provides a wide variety of activities. Beyond the well-known Las Vegas Strip, it's a great neighborhood to visit since it offers a distinct side to the city.

View Lake Las Vegas and Henderson

Exploring Henderson in the vicinity of Lake Las Vegas offers a calmer and more beautiful alternative to the busy Las Vegas Strip. A thorough guide to help you get the most out of your visit is provided below:

1. Henderson's Best

- **Henderson Bird Viewing Preserve:** Start your day with a trip to this tranquil natural environment, which has walking paths and a wide range of bird species. It's the ideal location for taking in the tranquil surroundings and birding.
- **Clark County Museum:** Visit the Clark County Museum to learn more about the history and

culture of the area. Investigate historical displays, such as a recreation of a street with authentic structures.

2. Las Vegas Lake

- **Lake Las Vegas:** Visit this lovely oasis in the middle of breathtaking desert vistas that are close by. You may engage in a variety of activities here:

- **Water Sports:** To explore the calm lake waters, you may rent a kayak, paddleboard, or pedal boat. Other well-liked choices include water skiing and wakeboarding.

- **Golf:** Play a round of golf at the acclaimed Reflection Bay Golf Club, which has beautiful lake vistas.

- **Village Shopping:** Browse the quaint stores, eateries, and marina in the Mediterranean-style Village at Lake Las Vegas.

- **Montelago Village:** Unwind in this Mediterranean-style neighborhood where you may eat at lakeside eateries, indulge in gelato, or just relax.

3. Parks & Recreation in Henderson

- **Ethel M Chocolates and Botanical Cactus Garden:** Explore the lovely Botanical Cactus Garden and the adjoining Ethel M Chocolates facility. Free examples of chocolate are likewise accessible.
- **Acacia Park:** Acacia Park offers picnic spots, playgrounds, and sports fields for a family-friendly visit.

4. Outdoor Activities

- **Hiking:** Sloan Canyon National Conservation Area, which is close by, has many hiking trails that Henderson visitors may take advantage of. The Petroglyph Canyon Trail, noted for its prehistoric rock art, should not be missed.
- **Mountain Biking:** If you like riding your bike on the mountainous terrain, check out the routes

around Bootleg Canyon, a well-known biking destination.

5. Grass Valley

- **Green Valley Ranch Resort:** Located in Henderson, Nevada, the Green Valley Ranch Resort and Spa is a five-star hotel and casino. Enjoy a meal at one of its elegant restaurants, chill in the spa, or laze by the pool.

6. Cultural Pursuits

- **Henderson Events Plaza:** Find out what events and concerts are taking place there. It is a lively community area with a variety of events all year long.

7. National Recreation Area in Lake Mead

- **Lake Mead:** If you have extra time, think about visiting Lake Mead, the country's biggest reservoir. You may go boating, on a picturesque drive, or to the adjacent Hoover Dam.

With options for water recreation, cultural discovery, and a refreshing diversion from the standard Las Vegas experience, Henderson and Lake Las Vegas provide a welcome change of pace. Anyone may enjoy this location, whether they are interested in nature, history, or just relaxing.

Discover the West Side

Discovering Las Vegas' West Side offers a distinctive mix of leisure, retail, and cultural attractions. Here is a comprehensive guide to help you explore this energetic area of the city:

1. National Conservation Area in Red Rock Canyon

- **Scenic Drive:** Visit Red Rock Canyon to kick off your West Side excursion. Drive the 13-mile scenic route and enjoy the breathtaking rock formations and arid surroundings. Don't forget to take pictures from different vantage points.
- **Hiking and Climbing:** Red Rock Canyon has a variety of hiking paths for hikers of all

experience levels. On its characteristic sandstone cliffs, you may also take pleasure in rock climbing.

2. Urban Summerlin

- **Shopping:** For shopping, visit Downtown Summerlin, a renowned area for both eating and shopping. Discover a range of boutiques, stores, and high-end brands.
- **Dining:** Indulge in a lunch at one of the numerous cafés and restaurants. From casual to gourmet eating, the neighborhood provides a variety of gastronomic alternatives.
- **City National Arena:** Visit City National Arena, the Vegas Golden Knights NHL team's practice space. You could see a hockey game or practice.

3. The Ballpark in Las Vegas

- **Minor League Baseball:** Attend a game at the Las Vegas Ballpark if you're a lover of the sport. The Oakland Athletics' Triple-A affiliate Las Vegas Aviators call it home.

4. Various Cultural Attractions

- **Beady Eye Art Gallery:** Take a look at the Beady Eye Art Gallery, which showcases jewelry, crafts, and modern and native art.
- **Bruce Trent Park:** Unwind in Bruce Trent Park, a popular venue for community activities like outdoor concerts and art exhibits.

5. Village of Tivoli

- **Shopping and Dining:** Tivoli Village is a retail and eating attraction with a European flair. Enjoy international food while strolling around the cobblestone walkways, visiting boutique stores, and shopping.

6. Nightlife and Entertainment

- **Red Rock Casino Resort & Spa:** This establishment provides a variety of eating, entertainment, and gaming opportunities. Attend a live show, try your luck at the casino, or eat at one of the establishments' restaurants.

- **Regal Red Rock & IMAX**: If you like watching movies, Regal Red Rock & IMAX is a great place to do it.

7. The Fireside Lounge and The Peppermill Restaurant

- **Iconic Dining:** Enjoy a meal at the Peppermill Restaurant and Fireside Lounge in Vegas, a famous restaurant and bar famed for its vintage decor and ample quantities.

8. Regional Parks

- **Parks:** Take leisurely walks, picnics, and outdoor activities at nearby parks including Bruce Trent Park and The Paseos Park.

A wide variety of activities are available on the West Side of Las Vegas, from the scenic Red Rock Canyon to the eating, shopping, and entertainment options in Downtown Summerlin. This area of the city offers activities for all types of travelers, whether they want to explore the great outdoors, engage in cultural pursuits, or just take in the local culture.

Tour Red Rock Canyon and Summerlin

Discovering Summerlin and Red Rock Canyon in Las Vegas provides a fantastic mix of outdoor recreation, shopping, eating, and natural beauty. A thorough guide to help you get the most out of your visit is provided below:

1. National Conservation Area in Red Rock Canyon

- **Scenic Drive:** The 13-mile scenic drive in Red Rock Canyon is a great place to start your vacation. Observe the distinctive desert scenery, which is distinguished by imposing red sandstone structures, in awe-inspiring detail.
- **Hiking and Climbing:** Red Rock Canyon has a wide variety of hiking paths for hikers of all experience levels. You may choose a path to fit your interests whether you're a newbie or

seasoned hiker. Popular options include the Ice Box Canyon Trail and the Calico Tanks Trail.

- **Rock Climbing:** This region is a rock climber's delight. Some of the greatest climbing chances in the world may be found in Red Rock Canyon.

2. Basin of Calico

- **Petroglyphs:** Calico Basin is located just outside Red Rock Canyon. Wander along the short route to see prehistoric Native American petroglyphs.

3. Urban Summerlin

- **Shopping:** For shopping, visit Downtown Summerlin, a renowned retail area. Explore a variety of stores, from well-known chains to one-of-a-kind boutiques. The setting is ideal for some shopping therapy.
- **Dining:** Indulge in a variety of gastronomic delights at the area's many eateries. Choices incorporate both relaxed and high end food.

4. Red Rock Resort & Casino

- **Gaming and Entertainment:** Try your luck at the casino if you're feeling fortunate. Additionally, the resort organizes live performances, concerts, and events.
- **Dining:** Indulge in a meal at one of the resort's restaurants, which serve a wide range of cuisines.

5. State Park at Spring Mountain Ranch

- Visit the historical ranch home and gorgeous surroundings at Spring Mountain Ranch State Park, a popular tourist destination. Learn about its history on a guided tour, then have a picnic in the picturesque location.

6. Cultural Encounters

- **Beady Eye Art Gallery:** Take a look around the Beady Eye Art Gallery, which features jewelry, crafts, and modern and native art.

7. Golf Courses Close by

- **Golfing:** Several golf courses, including TPC Las Vegas and Angel Park Golf Club, are located in the region. Golfers may tee off while admiring breathtaking desert scenery.

8. Taking a Relaxing Swim

- **Resort Pools:** Make use of the tempting pools and cabanas if you're staying at a nearby resort. It's a wonderful way to relax and enjoy the sunshine.

9. Authentic Beauty

- **Sunset Viewing:** If you want a unique experience, think about going to Red Rock Canyon to see the sunset. The sandstone structures' shifting hues are extremely mesmerizing.

10. Visitor's Center for Red Rock Canyon

- **Information:** Start your tour at the Red Rock Canyon Visitor Center for information. Maps, route details, and information on the local animals and geology are all available here.

Summerlin and Red Rock Canyon have plenty to offer everyone, whether you're an outdoor enthusiast, a shopper, or someone looking for leisure.

CHAPTER 4: ENTERTAINMENT AND GAMING

There is something for every taste and style in Las Vegas' illustrious and diversified gaming and entertainment industry. Here is a quick summary:

1. Casinos: The world-class casinos in Las Vegas are well-known. Play poker, blackjack, roulette, and other games to see if you can win some money. The Bellagio, Caesars Palace, and Venetian are three well-known casinos.

2. Shows and Performances: Enjoy breathtaking live performances, including Broadway-style musicals, magic shows, and comedy acts. The renowned Cirque du Soleil shows are not to be missed.

3. Nightclubs: With the best DJs, celebrity sightings, and spectacular dance floors, Las Vegas is home to some of the greatest nightclubs in the world. Famous clubs include OMNIA at Caesars Palace and XS at Encore.

4. Concerts and Events: Check out the entertainment schedule for events by well-known bands and performers. Major athletic and musical competitions are held in the city.

5. Sports Betting: If you like sports, you may place a wager at one of the many sportsbooks located within the casinos. As you sip beverages and place bets, watch your favorite sports on large screens.

6. Comedy Clubs: Have a good time at comedy clubs where both well-known and up-and-coming comedians perform.

7. Bars and Lounges: Las Vegas has a wide variety of pubs and lounges to fit every mood. Here, you may choose between a traditional cocktail lounge and a hip rooftop bar.

8. Adult Entertainment: Burlesque performances and adult revues are popular forms of adult entertainment in Las Vegas.

9. Escape Rooms: Escape rooms provide a thrilling and immersive experience for individuals who like riddles and challenges.

10. Virtual Reality: A few locations provide virtual reality experiences that let you enter a different world or test your gaming prowess.

Las Vegas is known as the entertainment center of the world, and it lives up to this title by providing tourists looking for fun and excitement with a broad variety of activities and experiences.

A Gambling Beginner's Guide

1. Know the Legal Gambling Age: In Las Vegas, you must be at least 21 years old to bet. Be aware of the

Legal Gambling Age. Bring proper identification from the government to show your age.

2. Set a Budget: Create a budget for your gaming activities before you begin to gamble. Follow this spending plan and go without pursuing misfortunes.

3. Learn the Games: Take some time to familiarize yourself with the regulations of the games you're interested in if you're new to gambling. Typical casino games consist of:

- **Slot Machines:** Slot machines are the simplest to use. Put your money in, hit the button, and cross your fingers that the symbols match.
- **Blackjack:** A card game in which the object is to have a hand higher than the dealer's without exceeding 21.
- **Poker:** From Texas Hold'em to Omaha, there are many different poker games available in Las Vegas. Before you sit at a table, learn the fundamentals.

- **Roulette:** Place a wager on the location of a ball's landing on a rotating wheel. It's an unpredictable game.
- **Craps:** A dice game in which bets are placed on the results of one or more rolls.

4. Start Small: If you've never gambled before, start with lower-risk games like slots. By doing so, you may experience the atmosphere of a casino without taking a significant financial risk.

5. Manage Your Bankroll: Divide your gaming budget across sessions to better manage your bankroll. Avoid the temptation to use money set aside for another session if you go over your budget for one session.

6. Take Advantage of Rewards: Join the casino's player's club or loyalty program to take advantage of rewards. Your gaming activities might earn you benefits like free play, meals, or hotel stays.

7. Learn Casino Etiquette: Each game has its own etiquette, so learn casino etiquette. To prevent any social errors, pay attention to other players and follow their example.

8. Stay Sober: While enjoying a drink while gaming is customary, too much alcohol might impair your judgment. Recognize your limitations and drink sensibly.

9. Practice Responsible Gambling: Gambling responsibly is important; if you believe it is becoming a problem, get assistance. Resources are available in Las Vegas for those with gambling addictions.

10. Have Fun: Enjoy yourself, and keep in mind that gambling is a sort of enjoyment. The main objective is to have fun, win or lose.

Slot machines and high-stakes poker tournaments are just two of the many types of gambling activities available in Las Vegas. You may get the most out of your urban gambling experience by beginning small, understanding the game, and handling your money sensibly. Enjoy your stay in the center of gaming!

Play Some Blackjack for Luck

Basics of Blackjack

In Las Vegas, one of the most played casino card games is blackjack, usually referred to as 21. The goal is to defeat the dealer by having a hand value that is closer to 21 than it is above it.

Starting

- **Locate a Table:** In the casino, look for a Blackjack table. Choose a table based on its minimum and maximum bet limits to fit your budget.
- **Purchase Chips:** At the table, trade in your cash for chips. Cash cannot be paid directly to the dealer.
- **Making a Bet:** Make your wager in the space provided in front of your seat.

Wallet Value

- The face value of number cards (2–10).

- King, Queen, and Jack face cards are awarded 10 points.

- Depending on which value helps your hand most, aces might be either 1 or 11 points.

Gameplay

- **Dealing the Cards:** Two cards are dealt to the dealer and each player. The dealer's cards normally have one face up (the "upcard") and one face down (the "hole card"), whereas the player's cards are typically face up.

- **Player's Turn:** During each player's turn, they must choose whether to "hit" (get a new card) or "stand" (retain their present hand). To go as close to 21 as you can without going over is the objective.

- **Dealer Turn:** After each player has finished taking their turn, the dealer then exposes their hole card. The dealer must adhere to certain guidelines. Typically, they must hit until they have at least 17 points in their hand and must stand on 17 or higher.

Payouts and Winnings

- You win if your hand comes closest to 21 without exceeding it in comparison to the dealer's.
- Your chances of winning are often enhanced if your first two cards are a "Blackjack" (an Ace and a 10-value card).
- Winning bets are normally paid out 1:1, which means you get your original stake back plus the same amount in profits.

Protection and Side Wagers

- A few Blackjack variants let players place side bets or buy insurance in case the dealer gets a blackjack. Although they have various chances and approaches, they might provide excitement.

Different Blackjack Plays

- Blackjack is available in a variety of forms in Las Vegas, including single-deck, double-deck, and multi-deck variants. Rules for each could be a little bit different.

Etiquette

- Show respect for the dealer and other players by adhering to the fundamental rules of Blackjack. Do not use your phone or touch your cards after they have been dealt.

Strategies

- To play Blackjack well, you must base your choices on both your hand and the dealer's upcard. To aid gamers in honing their talents, a wealth of materials and publications are accessible.

Blackjack is a game of skill and strategy that may increase your odds of winning in addition to being a fun game of chance. It may be fun and gratifying to try your luck at blackjack in Las Vegas, regardless of your level of expertise.

Poker for Novices

Poker is a well-known card game that mixes psychology, strategy, and ability. Although there are numerous poker types, Texas Hold'em is one of the most popular in both casinos and home gaming.

Starting

- **Hand Rankings:** Learn the order of poker hands, from highest (Royal Flush) to lowest (High Card), by familiarizing yourself with the hand rankings.

- **The Dealer Button:** The "dealer button" in Texas Hold'em revolves in a clockwise direction after each hand. It establishes who posts the small and large blinds as well as the dealer position.

- **Blinds and Antes:** The small blind and large blind, which are two players' forced wagers, are placed before each hand in Texas Hold'em. Thus, a beginning pot is created.

Gameplay

- **Hole Cards:** Each participant is given two personal cards (known as "hole cards") that they alone may see.

- **Betting Rounds:** Pre-flop, flop, turn, and river are the four betting rounds in Texas Hold'em. During these rounds, players have the option to check, bet, fold, call, or raise.

- **Community Cards:** Five community cards, which are shared by all players, are dealt face-up in the middle of the table. To create the greatest hand, combine these cards with the hole cards.

- **Hand Rankings:** The pot is won by the player holding the best five-card hand. Rankings for hands include straights, flushes, pairs, and more.

Various forms of poker

- **Texas Hold'em:** The most well-liked poker variant in which each player receives two hole cards and combines them with five other community cards to form the strongest hand.

- **Omaha:** This variant of Texas Hold'em requires players to utilize precisely two of their four-hole cards in addition to the three community cards.

- **Seven-Card Stud:** Each player receives seven cards, three of which are face-down and four of which are face-up. The finest five-card hand must be created by players.

Simple Techniques for Novices

- **Beginning Hands:** Acquire knowledge of which opening hands to hold and which to fold. Your odds of winning rise if you have a solid opening hand.

- **Position:** Your approach is influenced by where you sit with the dealer button. Late positions are better since they are nearer the button.

- **Bluffing:** Bluffing is a feature of poker, although it should only be used sparingly. When it makes sense, depending on your hand and the board, to bluff.

- **Bankroll Management:** Establish and adhere to your loss thresholds. Avoid chasing losses.

- **Observation:** Keep an eye out for the tactics and playing styles of your rivals. Make use of this knowledge to your advantage.

Poker Protocol

- Show respect for other players by adhering to the rules of poker, such as not showing your hand if you've folded.

Poker online

- To practice and acquire expertise, many novices start playing poker online. PokerStars and 888 Poker are two well-known online poker rooms.

Poker competitions

- The buy-ins and blinds for poker events are predetermined. Small buy-in home games to large competitions like the World Series of Poker (WSOP) are all included.

Education Resources

- For novices wishing to further their abilities, books, online courses, and poker forums are excellent sources of information.

Poker is a skill- and strategy-based game that rewards persistence and training. Understanding the fundamentals and honing your poker abilities may make the game interesting and perhaps rewarding, whether you're playing with friends or in a casino.

The Slot Machine World

Overview of Slot Machines

Slot machines, sometimes referred to as "slots" or "pokies" (in Australia), are well-liked casino games that are renowned for their simplicity and possibility for large winnings. Both in actual casinos and online, they are the most popular casino games worldwide.

Slot Machine Operation

- **Reels and Symbols:** Traditional slot machines include spinning reels that contain a variety of symbols. Video displays are often seen in modern slots.

- **Paylines: On** the reels, winning combos might appear along paylines. At least one paylines might be chosen by the player.

- **Bet Size:** Before the reels begin to spin, players decide on their stake size. bigger stakes often result in bigger possible winnings.

- **Random Number Generator (RNG):** Slot results are selected using a random number generator (RNG), which guarantees fairness.

- **Symbols and Payouts:** Each symbol has a specified reward value. Wins are produced by combinations of matching symbols along a payline.

- **Wilds and Scatters:** Special symbols like wild and scatter may activate extra features or raise winning chances.

- **Bonus Rounds:** Several slot machines contain bonus rounds that provide players more spins, multipliers, or playable mini-games.

Slot Machine Types

- **Classic Slots:** Slot machines known as "classic" slots include straightforward gameplay and common symbols like fruits and sevens.
- **Video Slots:** Today's video slots make use of computer animations, visuals, and a variety of themes. They provide many extra features.
- **Progressive Jackpot Slots:** These feature jackpots that rise with each wager until a player wins, with prizes that might be completely altered.
- **3D Slots:** Slots with three-dimensional images, or 3D slots, improve the visual experience.
- **Fruit Machines:** These slots are quite common in the UK and often include skill-based elements like nudges and holds.

Playing Slot Machines

- **Set a Budget:** Before beginning to gamble, choose a budget and follow it strictly.
- **Choose Your Slot Wisely:** Make Smart Slot Selections by Being Aware of the Rules, Paytable, and Volatility of the Game.
- **Bet Responsibly:** Bet sensibly by never placing a wager that you cannot afford to lose.
- **Use Bonuses:** A lot of online casinos give you free spins and bonuses for slots. Use the benefit, but read the terms.
- **Randomness:** Since slot machine results are unpredictable, there is no certain winning approach.
- **Know When to Quit:** If you're having a bad day, think about taking a break or giving up.

Slot Machine Manners

- Show courtesy to the casino employees and other players. Wait for your turn, don't monopolize the machines, and observe proper conduct.

Internet Slots

- Online casinos provide a large selection of online slots. They provide comfort and a huge selection of games.

History of Slot Machines

- Charles Fey created the first slot machine in 1895, which had three reels and a variety of symbols.
- From mechanical to electronic and video-based variants, slot machines have seen tremendous evolution.

A fascinating and enjoyable kind of gambling is slot machines. Understanding how they operate and developing ethical gaming practices may increase your fun while lowering dangers, whether you play them in a casino or online. Always play within your means and in moderation.

Decoding Video Poker

Getting Started with Video Poker

Video poker is a well-liked casino game that blends aspects of both slots and regular poker. When played well, it is renowned for its simplicity, strategy, and comparatively high player return percentages.

How to Play Video Poker

- **Machine Interface:** Video poker machines have a similar machine interface to slot machines, but they show poker hands on the screen.

- **Game Variations:** Jack or Better is one of the most popular Video Poker game varieties, but there are other options as well.

- **Betting:** Players decide how many coins to wager every hand and the coin denomination they wish to use while betting.

- **Dealing:** Five cards are dealt by the machine when the bet is placed.

- **Hold and Discard:** The players decide which cards to "hold" (keep) and which to "discard."

- **Replacement:** New cards from the deck are used to replace any discards.
- **Payout:** The payment depends on the last hand and the paytable.

Hands in Video Poker

- The goal is to put together the finest poker hand you can. For example, pairs, three-of-a-kind, full houses, etc., are ranked according to traditional poker hand rankings.

Paytable

- A paytable is included on every Video Poker machine and it lists the rewards for various hands according to the player's wager.

Video Poker Techniques

- **Basic Strategy:** Follow a fundamental Video Poker strategy that specifies which cards to retain in various circumstances. This plan seeks to optimize the profit you anticipate.

- **Game Variations:** Different versions of Video Poker may use somewhat different strategies. Learning the appropriate strategy for the game you're playing is crucial.
- **Risk Management:** Use sensible bet management to increase winnings during hot streaks and decrease losses during cold streaks.
- **Practice:** Use free online games or mobile applications to hone your Video Poker abilities.

Common Variations of Video Poker

- **Jacks or Better: A** pair of Jacks or higher is required to win.
- **Deuces Wild:** All twos (deuces) function as wild cards, replacing other cards to form winning hands.
- **Double Bonus Poker:** Offers extra payments for certain four-of-a-kind hands in double bonus poker.
- **Joker Poker:** Includes a joker as a wild card to increase the number of winning combinations.

Video Poker Manners

- Show courtesy to the casino employees and other players. Wait for your turn, keep your voice down, and follow standard casino protocol.

Video Poker Online

- A variety of Video Poker games are available at online casinos, allowing players to play from the comfort of their own homes.

Video poker is popular among casino aficionados because it blends the excitement of poker with the ease of slot machines. Your chances of winning may be increased by learning the fundamental game mechanics, rules, and techniques. When playing Video Poker, always play within your means and your means.

Roulette, A Game Of Chance

Roulette Introduction

Roulette is a well-liked and recognizable casino game distinguished by its betting possibilities and rotating wheel. The name of the game is taken from the French term "roulette," which translates to "little wheel."

How to Play Roulette

- **The Roulette Wheel:** Depending on the form, the game centers around a spinning wheel with numbered pockets (often 37 or 38).

- **Betting Table:** Using their predictions of where the ball will fall, players put wagers on the betting table.

- **Betting Options:** There are many other ways to gamble, including wagering on certain numbers, colors, or sets of numbers.

- **Spinning the Wheel:** The croupier (casino dealer), after accepting bets, turns the wheel and lets fly a little ball in the opposite direction.

- **Ball Lands:** The winning result is decided when the ball loses motion and falls in one of the numbered pockets.

Roulette Variations

- **European Roulette:** European roulette has 37 pockets with the numbers 1 through 36 and one zero.

- **American Roulette:** American roulette has 38 pockets with the numbers 1 through 36, one zero, and two zeros.

- **French Roulette:** Similar to European roulette, French roulette often offers extra wagering possibilities like "La Partage" and "En Prison."

Roulette Wagers

Inside Bets: Bets placed within the grid on certain numbers or groupings of numbers.

- **Straight Bet:** Straight bets involve wagering only one number.

- **Split Bet:** Selecting two neighboring numbers for a wager.

- **Street Bet:** A wager on a trio of numbers in a row.

- **Corner Bet:** A block of four digits is the subject of a corner bet.

- **Six-Line Bet:** A six-number wager on two adjacent rows is known as a six-line wager.

Outside Bets: Bets made on more general outcomes like groupings of colors or numbers.

- **Red/Black:** Making a wager on the hue of the victor's pocket.

- **Odd/Even:** Choosing whether to wager on an odd or an even number.

- **Dozen Bet:** A wager on a collection of 12 numbers (1–12, 13–24, and 25–36).

- **Column Bet:** Column betting is placing a wager on one of the three vertical columns.

Roulette Technique

- **Martingale:** A common betting strategy in which participants increase their wager after each loss to make up for prior losses with a single victory.

- **Fibonacci:** A technique that increases bets by a predetermined mathematical pattern and is based on the Fibonacci sequence.

- **D'Alembert:** A strategy in which stakes are raised after defeat and lowered following victory.
- **Labouchere:** Creating a list of numbers and placing a wager on the sum of the first and last numbers on the list is called labouchere.

Roulette Manners

- Respect the croupier and your fellow players.
- Only place bets when the dealer makes the appropriate announcement.
- As soon as the roulette wheel begins to turn, don't touch your bets or chips.
- When you win, tip the croupier.

Web-Based Roulette

- Different variations of Roulette are available at online casinos, enabling players to play in the convenience of their own homes.

Roulette is a beloved game in casinos all around the globe because it combines thrill and strategy. Understanding the different bet kinds and tactics might improve your experience playing Roulette, but you should never forget that it's a game of chance and that it's important to practice responsible gambling. Enjoy the excitement of seeing the ball land and the wheel spin in this well-known casino game.

Craps Made Easy

Getting Started with Craps

Craps is a well-liked dice-based casino game that offers a variety of betting opportunities and fast-paced action. Predicting the result of the roll of two six-sided dice is the goal of the game.

How to Play Craps

1. The Shooter: The shooter is the player who throws the dice in a live casino game.

2. Pass Line Bet: The majority of gamblers wager on the "Pass Line" or the "Don't Pass Line."

- **Pass Line Bet:** If the shooter's initial roll, or the come-out roll, is a 7 or an 11, you win. On 2, 3, or 12, you lose.

- **Don't Pass Line Bet:** The alternative to a Pass Line wager. Win or lose depending on 2, 3, or 11.

3. The Come-Out Roll: The come-out roll is the first dice throw made at the start of a betting round.

4. Point Numbers: If a 4, 5, 6, 8, 9, or 10 is rolled on the come-out roll, that number is designated as the "point."

5. Rolls After That: The shooter keeps rolling until they either land on the point number (winning for Pass Line bets) or land on a 7 (losing for Pass Line bets).

6. Other Bets: Craps offers a wide range of extra wagers, including Place Bets, Field Bets, and Proposition Bets.

Different Craps Bets

- **Pass Line Bet:** A wager that the shooter will prevail.
- **Don't Pass Line Bet:** Betting against the shooter on the don't pass line.
- **Come Bet:** After the come-out roll, put a wager similar to the Pass Line bet.

- **Don't Come Bet:** Similar to the Don't Pass Line wager, the Don't Come wager is made after the come-out roll.
- **Place Bets:** Make a wager that a certain number will be rolled before a 7 (4, 5, 6, 8, 9, or 10).
- **Field Bet:** A wager on how the dice will land on the next roll, usually on 2, 3, 4, 9, 10, 11, or 12.
- **Proposition Bets:** One-roll wagers on certain outcomes, like the "Any Craps" or "Hardway" bets, are known as proposition wagers.

Craps Approach

- **Pass Line and Come Bets:** The minimal house edge of the pass line and come bets makes them suitable for new players.
- **Don't Pass and Don't Come Bets:** The chances of the don't pass and don't come bets are a little better, but they may not be as common.
- **Place Bets:** For more frequent victories, wagering on 6 or 8 is typical.

- **Odds Bets:** To boost your chances of winning, add "Odds" bets wherever you can to your Pass Line or Come bets.

Craps Protocol

- Show courtesy to other players and the shooter.
- When it's your time, place your bets swiftly.
- When the dice are rolling, keep your hands and your chips off the table.
- Don't be superstitious; the result is just a matter of luck.

Gambling Online

- Craps is a game that may be played without going to a real-world casino since it is available at many online casinos.

A fun and sociable casino game that blends chance and technique is craps. Players may progressively explore more complicated bets as they grow used to the rules once they have a firm understanding of the fundamental bets and how the game works. At the Craps table, take pleasure in the excitement of the dice and the friendship.

Baccarat, A Staple Of The Casino

Getting Started With Baccarat

Baccarat is a well-known card game that is often connected to class and big stakes. The goal of the game is to place wagers on the results of two hands, the "Player" and the "Banker," to determine whose hand's total value will be the closest to 9.

How to Play Baccarat

1. Wallet Values

- The face value of the number cards (2–9) is valid.
- Face cards (King, Queen, and Jack) and 10s have no value.
- Points are awarded for aces.

2. Gameplay

- Baccarat is often played with several shuffled decks of cards.

- There are two hands in each round: the "Player" and the "Banker."
- The player's hand, the banker's hand, or a tie are the three possible wagers.

3. Making a Deal

- The Banker and the Player both get two cards, which are dealt face-up.
- Based on particular criteria that specify whether a "third card" is drawn, a third card may be handed. These guidelines are automatically followed without any input from the participants.

4. Calculating the Score

- The winning hand has a total value that is closest to 9.
- If the sum is more than 9, just the final digit is taken into account (15 becomes 5).
- A natural victory happens when either the Player or the Banker's opening two cards have a total of 8 or 9.

5. Payouts and Winnings

- Winning an even money wager on the right hand (Player or Banker).
- Although it is less prevalent, betting on a tie often has a bigger payoff.

Various Baccarat Wagers

- **Player Bet:** Betting on the outcome of the player's hand.
- **Banker Bet:** Putting money on the banker's hand to win.
- **Tie Bet:** A wager that the sum of the two hands will be the same.
- **Pair Bet:** A wager that either the Player or the Banker will get a pair of the first two cards dealt to them.

Baccarat Technique

- There are few methods in baccarat since it is mostly a game of luck.

- When placing bets, many players follow trends, such as monitoring previous results ("roadmaps").
- To prevent accumulating too many losses, it's crucial to control your bankroll and establish restrictions.

Various Baccarat Variations

- **Mini-Baccarat:** Mini-Baccarat is a condensed and accelerated variation of baccarat that is often played in casinos.
- **Punto Banco:** The most popular variation of Baccarat, particularly in North America, is played in casinos.

Web-Based Baccarat

- There are many variations of Baccarat available at online casinos, including live dealer games where actual dealers control the cards through video streaming.

An attractive and simple card game noted for its elegance and simplicity is baccarat. Playing online or at an opulent casino gives excitement and the chance to engage in low- and high-stakes gambling. By mastering the fundamentals of baccarat, you can fully appreciate this time-honored casino game.

Place Sports Bets Like a Pro

If done correctly, sports betting can be thrilling and even rewarding. Here is a detailed tutorial on how to wager on sports like a pro:

1. Recognize the Fundamentals

- Become familiar with the sports you wish to wager on. Find out about the players, teams, and recent results.

2. Bankroll Control

- Establish a spending limit for your wagering on sports. Never risk cash that you can't bear to lose.

- To limit risk, divide your money into units (usually 1-5% every wager).

3. How to Choose the Best Odds

- For the same event, different bookmakers provide different odds. Search for the greatest deal at all times.
- Line shopping has a long-term, considerable influence on your profitability.

4. Variety of Bets

- **Moneyline:** Place a wager on the game's winner using odds that take favorites and underdogs into account.
- **Point Spread:** Place a wager on either the favorite to win by a certain margin or the underdog to lose by a smaller margin.
- **Over/Under (Totals):** Place a wager on whether the final score will exceed or fall short of a certain amount.

- **Proposition Bets (Props):** Bet on certain game-related occurrences (such as player statistics).
- **Parlays:** For bigger returns but more risk, combine many bets onto a single ticket.

5. Research and Handicap

- Examine team statistics, recent performance, injuries, and other variables that may have an impact on the result.
- Take into account the handicap (point spread) and its effects.

6. Bankroll Management

- Put into action a staking strategy depending on the amount of your money and your risk tolerance.
- Refrain from chasing losses by placing higher bets to rapidly make up losses.

7. Respect Your Emotions

- Avoid letting your emotions influence your betting choices. Keep to your plan and study.

- Refrain from placing bets on your preferred team out of pure devotion.

8. Line Motion

- Pay attention to how the line moves; it might show you where the sharp bettors are leaning.

- If you think the odds will be in your favor, think about putting your bets early.

9. Control Several Sportsbooks

- Accessing the greatest odds and promos is made possible by having accounts with many sportsbooks.

- Verify the reputation and legitimacy of the sportsbooks you choose.

10. Keep Records

- Keep track of every wager you make, noting the date, the kind of wager, the odds, the stake, and the result.

- Examining prior wagers might help you pinpoint the advantages and disadvantages of your approach.

11. Stay Up to Date

- Stay current on news, injuries, and other events that can affect your wagers.

- Pay attention to professional advice, but make your well-informed conclusions.

12. Keep Your Discipline

- Adhere to your plan and avoid veering off course because of rash judgments.

- Keep your bet sizes constant; don't raise them following victories.

13. Accept Variance

- Recognize that losses are a part of sports betting; even experienced gamblers go through losing streaks.
- Exercise patience and confidence in your long-term plan.

14. Prudent Gambling

- If you ever feel that sports betting is having a detrimental impact on your life or money, get assistance and think about your options for self-exclusion.

Professional sports betting involves focus, preparation, and a calculated strategy. You can make sports betting a fun and perhaps lucrative pastime by managing your money intelligently, keeping up to date, and following a consistent plan.

Discover The City's Best Casinos

1. Casino and Hotel in Bellagio

- The Bellagio is recognized for its elegance and opulence and is situated on the well-known Las Vegas Strip.
- Take in the magnificent fountain display in front of the hotel.
- A variety of table games, slot machines, and poker rooms are available at the casino.

2. Casino and Resort at The Venetian
- Take a gondola ride around the canals of Venice in Las Vegas.
- The casino offers a wide variety of table games, slot machines, and sporting events.

3. Hotel and Casino MGM Grand
- It boasts one of the biggest gaming areas of any hotel in the world.
- Check out the lively poker room, slots, and table games.
- Attend the fun performances at the MGM Grand Garden Arena.

4. Caesars Palace

- A recognizable landmark in Las Vegas that has Roman-inspired architecture.
- The casino has a poker area and many other gambling opportunities.
- The complex offers upscale shopping and exquisite eating.

5. Las Vegas' Wynn

- This luxurious resort provides a high-end gambling experience.
- Check out the high-stakes poker room, slots, and table games.
- Take in the picturesque Wynn Golf Club and the lovely Lake of Dreams.

6. Resort and Casino ARIA

- The casino at ARIA is renowned for its cutting-edge aesthetic and energetic ambiance.
- Discover a wide selection of slot machines, table games, and a high-limit lounge.

- The resort also has top-notch dining options and a vibrant nightlife.

7. The Las Vegas Cosmopolitan

- A chic casino in a fashionable, contemporary resort.
- Enjoy the Marquee nightclub and table and slot games.
- The rooftop pool, which offers breathtaking views of the Strip, is a must-see.

8. Casino and Resort at The Palazzo

- This opulent resort, which is connected to The Venetian, provides a comparable gaming experience.
- Look at a range of gaming possibilities and luxury retail.

9. Macau's Wynn

- Located in Macau, which is often referred to as the "Monte Carlo of the East."

- This casino resort combines luxury with Asian-inspired architecture.
- Play slots and table games, and savor exquisite eating selections.

10. Singapore's Marina Bay Sands

- One of the most recognizable casinos in the world, with a stunning rooftop pool.
- The casino provides a broad range of gambling opportunities, including baccarat and slot machines.
- Discover posh stores, eateries, and the breathtaking SkyPark.

11. Monaco's Casino de Monte-Carlo

- At this storied casino, enjoy the sophistication of European gaming.
- Participate in age-old table games including poker, blackjack, and roulette.
- Take in the opulent structures from the Belle Époque.

12. Macao's The Venetian

- A component of Macau's biggest casino complex.
- Has a huge gaming area with a lot of tables and slot machines.
- Take in the entertainment, shopping, and architecture in the Venetian style.

13. The Sydney Star

- The best casino in Australia is in Sydney.
- Offers a variety of table games, poker, and video gaming devices.
- Delight in exquisite food and live performance.

Always play sensibly and within your means. Casinos are an exciting component of every city's nightlife since they provide a variety of activities outside of gaming, such as shows and excellent cuisine.

CHAPTER 5: PERFORMANCES & SHOWS IN LAS VEGAS

The city's entertainment culture is dominated by the shows and acts in Vegas. Here is a quick summary:

1. Cirque du Soleil

- Noted for its stunning acrobatic feats and creative productions.
- Iconic performances include "O" at Bellagio and "Michael Jackson ONE" at Mandalay Bay.

2. Magic Shows

- View mind-blowing magic performances by renowned illusionists like Penn & Teller and David Copperfield.

3. Musical Acts

- Attend performances by notable musicians, including pop artists and renowned bands.

4. Comedy Clubs

- Laughter is guaranteed in comedy clubs where stand-up comedians perform.

5. Broadway Productions

- A number of the top Broadway shows go to Las Vegas.

6. Impersonators

- From Frank Sinatra to Elvis Presley, Vegas is home to numerous impersonators of famous people.

7. Adult Revues

- There are alternatives like "Absinthe" and burlesque revues for more adult-oriented entertainment.

8. Hypnosis and Mentalism

- With the help of hypnotists and mentalists, explore the secrets of the mind.

9. Tribute Concerts

- Tribute concerts honor renowned musicians and performers and provide a nostalgic experience.

10. Dinner Shows

- At dinner theaters with a variety of themes, you may enjoy both a meal and entertainment.

Las Vegas offers a wide variety of events and performances to fit every preference, whether you like music, magic, comedy, or something completely different. Always reserve tickets in advance for popular performances.

Arrange a Night Out

1. Pick Your Entertainment

- Start the evening off by picking a concert, performance, or event.
- Take into account possibilities like Cirque du Soleil, magic shows, comedy clubs, and concerts.

2. Dining Reservations

- Reserve a table for supper at a restaurant that appeals to you.
- Vegas boasts top-notch eating options, including buffets and restaurants with famous chefs.

3. Pre-Show Beverages

- The Strip is filled with establishments that provide specialty beverages and breathtaking views. Enjoy pre-show cocktails at a hip club or bar.

4. Attend Your Selected Event

- Go to the performance or show of your choice.
- For popular shows in particular, get there early to get decent seats.

5. Post-Show Fun

- After the event, take advantage of the exciting nightlife.
- To keep the fun going, visit nightclubs, rooftop bars, or casinos.

6. Casino Time

- If you want to gamble, visit one of the renowned casinos in the area. Play roulette, blackjack, poker, or slots.

7. Late-Night Eats

- Fill up on a late-night snack.
- Certain eateries are open around the clock and provide a range of cuisines.

8. Transportation

- Arrange your return trip to your lodging.
- There are plenty of taxis, rideshares, and hotel shuttles available.

9. Dress Code

- Pay attention to the attire requirements in fancy restaurants and clubs.
- Be sure to verify the exact criteria and dress to impress.

10. Be Safe

- Although Vegas is renowned for its exciting nightlife, personal safety must always come first.
- Be mindful of your surroundings and use alcohol sensibly.

11. Group Activities

- If you're traveling in a group, think about scheduling a VIP experience at a nightclub. Some places provide bottle service and reserved seats.

There are several possibilities to have a special night out in Las Vegas. Planning prepared assures a memorable evening in the Entertainment Capital of the World, whether you're celebrating, looking for entertainment, or trying your luck at the tables.

Take In Some Afternoon Entertainment

1. Afternoon Performances: There are several afternoon performances available in Las Vegas. Consider going to a popular production's matinee, such as a magic show or comedy act. Since matinee performances could have constrained scheduling, check showtimes and availability beforehand.

2. Cirque du Soleil: In the early evening, take in one of the legendary Cirque du Soleil performances like "Michael Jackson ONE" or "O." Acrobatics, music, and visual effects are all used in these spellbinding shows.

3. Piano Bars and Lounges: There are piano bars and lounges at many hotels where live music is played in the afternoon. Drink drinks while taking in the music of gifted pianists or small bands.

4. High Tea: A few upmarket hotels provide afternoon high tea services. Enjoy an exquisite environment while indulging in a variety of teas, finger sandwiches, pastries, and desserts.

5. Poolside Relaxation: Spend your day at the pool if you're staying at a resort. Enjoy the pool, the sun, and the cool beverages from the poolside bars.

6. Art Galleries: Explore the Strip's art galleries and exhibits. Take in the classic and modern works of art, which are often located within the hotels themselves.

7. Spa Services: If you want to unwind, schedule an afternoon spa visit. Relax with massages, facials, and other wellness procedures in opulent spas.

8. Shopping: Vegas is a retail mecca, spend the day perusing upscale boutiques, specialty shops, and retail outlets. Numerous retail centers, including the Forum Shops at Caesars Palace, combine entertainment and shopping.

9. Watching Sports: If you like sports, go to a sports bar to watch a game. Sports clubs in Las Vegas with large screens are ideal for watching an afternoon game.

10. Afternoon Tea Dance: A few locations organize tea dances that include music, dancing, and small bites. For afternoon dancing possibilities, check the local events calendar.

11. Sightseeing Tours: Make the most of the pleasant afternoon weather by going on a sightseeing tour. There are bus trips, chopper rides, and escorted city tours available.

12. Outdoor Activities: Take part in outdoor activities like strolls along the Las Vegas Strip or hiking in the neighboring Red Rock Canyon.

13. Gambling: If you want to gamble, check out the casinos. Evenings may not be as packed as the afternoon.

Every taste may be satisfied by the variety of entertainment alternatives in Las Vegas. In this energetic city, there are lots of afternoon activities to keep you occupied, whether you like relaxing or engaging entertainment.

Attend Evening Shows

You're in for a treat if you want to see a nighttime revue in Las Vegas.

1. Cirque du Soleil: The Cirque du Soleil shows in Las Vegas are well-known. Acrobatics, music, and visual effects in shows like "O" at Bellagio and "Michael Jackson ONE" at Mandalay Bay are astounding. Because these performances often sell out, be sure to get your tickets in advance.

2. Magic Shows: Experience an evening of mystery and wonder at a magic performance by a well-known magician, such as Penn & Teller at the Rio or David Copperfield at the MGM Grand. Be ready to be astounded by astounding illusions and deception.

3. Comedy Clubs: Have a good time at a comedy club in Vegas. Talented comedians may be found in The Comedy Cellar at the Rio and Brad Garrett's Comedy Club at the MGM Grand. These places often feature a variety of stand-up comedians.

4. Burlesque and Cabaret: Attend burlesque and cabaret performances to see seductive and intriguing acts. Sensual comedy, acrobatics, and burlesque are all combined in performances like "X Burlesque" at the Flamingo and "Absinthe" at Caesars Palace.

5. Tribute Shows: Honor iconic musicians with tribute performances. At Tropicana, "Legends in Concert" exhibits skilled impersonators playing renowned stars. Enjoy your favorite performers' songs and memories.

6. Variety Shows: Las Vegas offers a wide range of performances that include humor, music, and original talents. The roster for "V - The Ultimate Variety Show" at Planet Hollywood is varied. For those who like a little bit of everything, these programs are ideal.

7. Adult Shows: If you're looking for bold and risqué entertainment for adults, check out Cirque du Soleil's "Zumanity" at New York-New York. These programs challenge conventions and provide a more sensuous experience.

8. Dinner Shows: Dinner shows combine a meal with entertainment. The Excalibur's "Tournament of Kings" and "Medieval Times" transport you to a bygone era when knights and kings reigned. Watch live jousting and entertainment while indulging in a substantial feast.

9. Live Music and Concerts: Attend live music performances and concerts at places like T-Mobile Arena, The Joint at Hard Rock Hotel, and The Colosseum at Caesars Palace. Top musical artists from a variety of genres come to Vegas.

10. Hypnosis and Mind-Reading: Watch hypnotism and mind-reading performances to get entranced. Intriguing encounters include "Marc Savard Comedy Hypnosis" at V Theater and "The Mentalist" at Planet Hollywood. See volunteers being hypnotized or experience mind-blowing mentalism for yourself.

11. Late-Night Performances: Extend the duration of your evening with late-night performances that begin beyond regular hours. Late-night entertainment is provided by "Opium" at The Cosmopolitan and "Murray the Magician" at Tropicana.

You may discover the ideal performance to make your night special at one of Las Vegas nighttime revues, which appeal to a broad variety of preferences. Make sure to reserve your tickets in advance, get there early, and get ready for a night of entertainment that can only be found in Las Vegas.

Learn About Local Headliners

An intriguing aspect of the city's entertainment culture is exploring the resident headliners.

1. Celine Dion: Celine Dion, one of the most well-known singers in the world, had a long-running successful residency at The Colosseum at Caesars Palace. A wonderful evening is guaranteed with her stirring performances and timeless favorites.

2. Elton John: Sir Elton John's "The Million Dollar Piano" residency was a highlight at Caesars Palace's Colosseum. His famed melodies and ostentatious theatrical presence were enjoyed by audiences.

3. Britney Spears: A pop culture icon Britney Spears performed her hit songs in a dynamic concert during her stay at Park Theater at Park MGM. Her performances included music, dancing, and stunning images.

4. Bruno Mars: Bruno Mars' Park Theater at Park MGM engagement displayed his extraordinary musical abilities. His songs, such as "Uptown Funk" and "Just the Way You Are," had the crowd moving.

5. Lady Gaga: Lady Gaga's Park Theater at Park MGM residency, "Enigma," merged her musical ability with cutting-edge theatrics. Her biggest hits were played throughout the event, which also highlighted her range as an artist.

6. Aerosmith: Rock royalty Aerosmith played at Park Theater at Park MGM as part of their "Deuces Are Wild" engagement. Rock songs from the band's long discography were loved by the audience.

7. Shania Twain: Shania Twain, a country-pop icon, performed at the Zappos Theater at Planet Hollywood as part of her "Let's Go!" engagement. Her greatest songs were performed in the fascinating theatrical play.

8. Rod Stewart: Rock and pop legend Rod Stewart's "Rod Stewart: The Hits" residency provided entertainment for crowds at The Colosseum at Caesars Palace. Fans loved his classic tunes.

9. Gwen Stefani: Gwen Stefani honored her career as a solo artist and No Doubt frontwoman during her residency, "Gwen Stefani - Just a Girl," at Zappos Theater at Planet Hollywood. Her trademark flair and hits were well-liked by audiences.

10. Donny and Marie Osmond: At the Flamingo in Las Vegas, Donny and Marie Osmond performed as part of their ongoing residency. The brother and sister team enchanted crowds with their music, humor, and nostalgia.

11. Legends in Concert: The Tropicana Las Vegas's "Legends in Concert" program offers amazing tribute performers that pay homage to iconic icons like Michael Jackson, Whitney Houston, and Elvis Presley.

There is something for everyone because of the variety of musical genres and entertainment styles offered by Las Vegas' resident superstars. Check the schedule and get your tickets in advance to see these legendary performers at the center of global entertainment.

Take In The Scene For Performing Arts

Finding the Performing Arts Scene in Las Vegas

Las Vegas has a thriving performing arts scene in addition to its casinos and nightlife. Here is a thorough explanation of how to do it:

1. Smith Center for the Performing Arts: The Smith Center is a major center for the arts in downtown Las Vegas. It is a must-see for theater fans since it presents Broadway plays, ballet, opera, and a variety of concerts.

2. Cirque du Soleil: With several performances taking place across the city, Cirque du Soleil is a household name in Las Vegas. A must-see performance is "O" at Bellagio, "Michael Jackson ONE" at Mandalay Bay, and "The Beatles LOVE" at The Mirage.

3. Broadway in the Hood: This community-based charity theatrical company presents interesting and varied plays. They often provide performances in the Smith Center, offering a real theatrical experience.

4. Cockroach Theatre: Cockroach Theatre, known for its cutting-edge and creative plays, introduces new and modern theater to the Vegas arts scene.

5. Majestic Repertory Theatre: Majestic Repertory Theatre is known for producing immersive and difficult plays that often address social and cultural issues.

6. The Space: This compact venue holds a range of events, such as cabaret shows, live music concerts, and comedy plays.

7. Super Summer Theatre: This outdoor theater provides a unique experience and is situated in the lovely Spring Mountain Ranch State Park. Enjoy summertime performances of Broadway musicals and outdoor concerts.

8. Las Vegas Philharmonic: Listen to the Las Vegas Philharmonic play a variety of symphonic masterworks to enjoy classical music at its best.

9. Jazz Clubs: The jazz culture in Las Vegas is expanding, with live jazz concerts taking place at places like The Dispensary Lounge and The Italian American Club.

10. Local Comedy Clubs: Have a good time laughing at places like The Comedy Cellar at the Rio and the renowned Laugh Factory in the Tropicana.

11. West Las Vegas Arts Center: This community center, which holds diverse cultural events and exhibits, is a great place to learn about African-American culture and art.

12. Art Galleries: Numerous art galleries in the downtown Arts District feature modern and local artists.

13. First Friday: The Arts District comes alive on the first Friday of every month with art exhibits, food trucks, live music, and other events.

14. Nevada Ballet Theatre: Take in performances of the Nevada Ballet Theatre, which are of the highest caliber.

The performing arts scene in Las Vegas provides a wide range of entertainment alternatives for cultural fans, including ballet, stand-up comedy, and Broadway successes in addition to avant-garde theater. To take advantage of the diverse selection of performances the city has to offer, be sure to check the event calendars and get your tickets in advance.

CHAPTER 6: EXCURSIONS FROM LAS VEGAS

Welcome To Side Trips

Las Vegas is known for its entertainment, but there are a lot of interesting side excursions that provide an escape from the city's flash and glitter. A deeper look at these thrilling outings is provided below:

1. The Grand Canyon: The Grand Canyon is a well-known natural marvel that captivates visitors with its breathtaking landscapes. Experience its spectacular splendor by exploring the South Rim, going on a helicopter trip, or riding a mule.

2. Hoover Dam: Located not far from Las Vegas, the Hoover Dam is a wonder of engineering. Explore its importance and history with guided tours, and don't forget to take in the expansive views from the Mike O'Callaghan-Pat Tillman Memorial Bridge.

3. Red Rock Canyon: A short distance from the city is Red Rock Canyon, which provides a striking contrast to the Las Vegas Strip. Learn about rock formations, hiking paths, and beautiful drives.

4. Valley of Fire State Park: Valley of Fire State Park is a photographer's dream because of its vivid red sandstone formations. Discover paths, awe at petroglyphs, and take in this desert wonder's natural splendor.

5. Lake Mead: The Hoover Dam built Lake Mead, a large reservoir that is ideal for water sports. Have fun kayaking, boating, or perhaps taking a trip in a paddlewheel boat.

6. Death Valley National Park: Explore Badwater Basin, the lowest point in North America, to see the distinctive desert vistas and explore artist's palettes for breathtaking views in Death Valley National Park.

7. Zion National Park: This Park is a hiker's paradise because of its majestic canyons and high sandstone cliffs, which are located a little outside of the city.

8. Bryce Canyon National Park: The hoodoos and natural amphitheaters of Bryce Canyon National Park make the extra travel worthwhile.

9. Ghost Towns: In Nevada's past, places like Rhyolite and Nelson are no longer inhabited. Investigate these historical artifacts to learn amazing tales.

10. Area 51: For the daring, take a tour of Area 51's enigmatic surroundings and learn about its otherworldly lore.

11. Route 66: Set off on a nostalgic adventure down the legendary Route 66, replete with amusing side-stops and vintage eateries.

12. Antelope Canyon and Horseshoe Bend: The ethereal grandeur of Antelope Canyon and the recognizable Horseshoe Bend are worth the travel into Arizona, despite the lengthier day excursion.

13. Joshua Tree National Park: It offers a distinctive desert environment where you may explore bizarre rock formations and enjoy nighttime stargazing.

These side excursions provide a wide variety of activities just beyond the neon lights of Las Vegas, whether you're looking for natural marvels, historical sites, or a little bit of adventure. Create enduring memories of your trip to the American Southwest by organizing your excursions, taking in the sights, and so on.

Arrange Your Vacations

1. Grand Canyon Journeys

- **South Rim:** With its expansive views and hiking routes, see one of the seven natural wonders of the world.

- **West Rim:** Visit the Grand Canyon Skywalk on the West Rim for breathtaking vistas and the opportunity to cross the canyon's rim.
- **North Rim:** Explore a more sedate, less populated region with breathtaking scenery and fantastic astronomy.

2. Exploration of the Hoover Dam

- Go on a guided tour to discover the history and importance of the dam's construction.
- For breathtaking pictures, cross the Mike O'Callaghan-Pat Tillman Memorial Bridge.

3. Escape from Red Rock Canyon

- Explore the vibrant red sandstone formations on foot or by bicycle.
- For breathtaking vistas, take the 13-mile scenic circle drive.

6. Journey to the Valley of Fire

- See ancient petroglyphs and blazing red rock formations.

- Look inside the White Domes and the Fire Wave for amazing geological marvels.

7. Lake Mead Excursions

- For fun on the water, rent a boat, kayak, or paddleboard.
- Ride a paddlewheel boat on Lake Mead for a leisurely tour.

8. Death Valley Finding

- Travel to Badwater Basin, North America's lowest point.
- Look through the Artist's Palette for vivid geological hues.

9. Travel to Zion National Park

- Take a hike into the Zion Narrows and amid spectacular sandstone cliffs.
- Drive into the park's interior on the picturesque route.

10. Investigation of Bryce Canyon

- Be in awe of the unusual hoodoos and on-site amphitheaters.
- For the greatest views, hike around the rim.

11. Ghost Town Journeys

- Visit historical sites like Rhyolite and Nelson.
- Take pictures of deteriorating buildings to learn their intriguing histories.

12. Interplanetary Encounters

- Set off on a tour of the enigmatic Area 51 with a guide.
- Investigate UFO mythology and take in the surreal setting.

13. Journey along Route 66

- Travel along Route 66's illustrious roadside attractions.
- Indulge in traditional diner fare and savor the Mother Road's nostalgia.

14. Excursion to Horseshoe Bend and Antelope Canyon

- Visit Antelope Canyon in Arizona to see its surreal beauty.
- Take in the breathtaking view of the Colorado River from the famed Horseshoe Bend.

15. Adventure in Joshua Tree National Park

- Explore the bizarre topography, distinctive rock formations, and Joshua trees.
- Take advantage of possibilities for stargazing with less light pollution.

Each vacation spot offers a distinctive fusion of the outdoors, culture, and adventure. These excursions will enrich your time in Las Vegas, whether you're searching for spectacular views, embracing history, or alien secrets. Make experiences that extend beyond the renowned Las Vegas Strip by planning and packing your sense of adventure.

Visit Mount Charleston

A vacation to Mount Charleston is the ideal getaway if you want to unwind in the splendor of nature while escaping the desert heat. This mountain sanctuary is close to Las Vegas and provides a wide range of outdoor activities. Here is a map for exploring Mount Charleston:

1. Drive Scenically

- Start your trip off with a gorgeous drive up Kyle Canyon Road, which is lined with imposing ponderosa pines.
- Take a break at designated sites for breathtaking Spring Mountain views.

2. Hiking Routes

- Lace up your hiking boots and choose from a variety of paths suitable for hikers of all experience levels.
- For a hard trek, try the North Loop Trail, which is recommended for seasoned hikers, or the intermediate Cathedral Rock Trail.

3. Picnic Locations

- Bring lunch, then unwind at one of the numerous shady picnic spots with tables and grills.

- Take in the pleasant mountain winds while you eat.

4. Camping Excursions

- Camp in well-known campsites like McWilliams or Fletcher View to extend your stay.

- Wake up to the wonderful symphony of nature after sleeping beneath the stars.

5. Snowboarding and Skiing (winter)

- Go skiing or snowboarding at the Las Vegas Ski and Snowboard Resort throughout the winter.

- Enjoy skiing and snowboarding within a short drive from the Strip.

6. Trail to Mary Jane Falls

- To access a magnificent waterfall (seasonal) in a beautiful alpine environment, hike the Mary Jane Falls Trail.

- Don't forget your camera; there are many great picture possibilities along this walk.

7. Mount Charleston Inn

- Visit the Mount Charleston Lodge for a hearty supper and stunning mountain views.
- Warm up with some hot chocolate in the winter or cool off on the outside patio in the summer.

8. Viewing Wildflowers in the Spring

- The region has a wildflower bloom in the spring. Be on the lookout for the vibrant blossoms.
- The greatest wildflower displays may be seen on Mt. Charleston's lower slopes.

9. Watching Birds

- To see local and migrating birds, bring your binoculars and a birding guide.
- Birdwatchers will find Mt. Charleston to be a sanctuary.

10. Peak in Charleston

- Charleston Peak, Clark County's highest peak, is a challenge for intrepid hikers.
- This strenuous hike will pay you with breathtaking 360-degree vistas.

11. Stargazing

- Take advantage of the astronomy opportunities as night comes.
- Bring a telescope or just spread out a blanket to see a spectacular cosmic display.

12. Autumn Fall Foliage

- Go during the autumn to see the aspens and maples' leaves change into a stunning tapestry of reds and yellows.
- A photographer's paradise, autumn.

Always check the weather before traveling since it might be quite different from Las Vegas in terms of temperature. Mt. Charleston provides a tranquil mountain hideaway that is always worth exploring, whether you're looking for adventure, leisure, or a vacation from the city lights.

Explore the Lake Mead Area's Beauty

The Lake Mead National Recreation Area, which is conveniently located near Las Vegas, entices visitors with its breathtaking scenery, clear waters, and variety of outdoor activities. Here is a guide to help you discover the Lake Mead region's beauty:

1. Lake Mead

- The Hoover Dam's creation, Lake Mead, is the ideal place to begin your trip.
- To explore the lake's wide breadth, which covers more than 150,000 acres, you may rent a boat, a kayak, or a paddle board.
- Striped bass, catfish, and other species may all be caught by anglers.

2. Holbrook Dam

- The legendary Hoover Dam is a work of engineering wonder that is open for guided visits.
- Cross the Pat Tillman and Mike O'Callaghan Memorial Bridge for sweeping vistas.

3. Railway Heritage Trail

- For a leisurely journey along the former rail line, hike or bike the Historic Railroad Trail.
- Discover the dam's history while taking in the breathtaking scenery.

4. Water Sports

- Participate in watersports including jet skiing, swimming, and water skiing.
- The lake's marinas provide equipment rentals and other services for a day on the water.

5. Desert Exploration

- Discover the Mojave Desert's surrounding area's arid beauty.

- Be alert for desert animals, such as bighorn sheep, coyotes, and many kinds of birds.

6. The Black Canyon Via kayak

- Canoe the scenic Black Canyon, which is a part of the Colorado River.
- Explore secret hot springs and admire the striking canyon cliffs.

7. Under the Stars Camping

- Camp out at one of the local campsites for a night (or more).
- Take pleasure in the tranquility of the desert night sky and the serene sounds of nature.

8. Hiking Routes

- Pick from a variety of hiking paths with varied degrees of difficulty.
- The Colorado River may be reached through the White Rock Canyon Trail for a cool plunge.

9. Visitor Center at Lake Mead

- For information about the history, animals, and geology of the region, stop by the Lake Mead Visitor Center.
- Park rangers are on hand to respond to inquiries and provide directions and information.

10. Birdwatching

- The variety of birds that live in the region will excite bird watchers.
- Bring your binoculars and a birding guide so you can view animals like bald eagles and desert bighorn sheep.

11. Enticing Drives

- For stunning lake views, go for a leisurely drive down Lake Shore Road.
- The Northshore Road provides access to several beaches as well as breathtaking views.

12. Lake Mead Overlook at Dusk

- Enjoy a stunning sunset at the Lake Mead Overlook to round off your day.
- The interplay of colors on the river and the scenery is breathtaking.

The Lake Mead region offers an oasis of unspoiled beauty in the Nevada desert, whether you're looking for a sea adventure, desert exploration, or just a peaceful vacation from the city. Both nature lovers and outdoor enthusiasts should visit this place.

Explore The Area 51 Mysteries

Area 51, a secret facility hidden deep in the Nevada desert, has captured the curiosity of tourists, UFO enthusiasts, and conspiracy theorists alike. The area around the covert military installation provides a distinctive and mysterious experience, but the base itself remains cloaked in mystery. How to go into the Area 51 enigma is as follows:

1. Rebecca, Nevada

- The unofficial entrance to Area 51 is the little village of Rachel, where your quest starts.
- Make a pit stop at the Little A'Le'Inn, a unique roadside inn and restaurant with UFO-themed décor.

2. Interplanetary Highway

- Travel down the Extraterrestrial Highway, also known as Nevada State Route 375.
- Take a picturesque trip over the barren desert areas, sometimes stopping to take in odd sights.

3. Center for Alien Research

- Pay a visit to the Alien Research Center, a store and resource center.
- Browse goods with an extraterrestrial theme and discover local legends about UFOs.

4. Border of Area 51

- Arrive at the famed Area 51's boundary, which is delineated by cautionary signs and security cameras.

- Take note that entering the base illegally or trying to do so will be closely watched.

5. The Tikaboo Peak

- Hike to Tikaboo Peak, which is roughly 26 miles away, to see a distant look at Area 51.

- Take a pair of binoculars or a telescope to see distant buildings and activities.

6. The Dark Postbox

- Visit the Black Mailbox, now white, which belonged to a rancher in the past and served as a gathering place for those interested in UFOs.

- Send a message to the mysterious "Cammo Dudes," the security guards that patrol Area 51, or go in search of them.

7. Night Sky-Watching

- Set a camp or go stargazing in the neighboring desert for a chance to see strange lights and celestial occurrences.

8. Experiences with Extraterrestrials

- Interact with locals and other visitors who recount their bizarre adventures.
- Participate in alien celebrations like the Alienstock festival.

9. Backcountry Tours with Rachel

- Join one of the Rachel residents' guided tours to learn more about Area 51's history and lore.

10. Maintain an Open Mind

- While Area 51's secrets continue to elude investigators, go into the encounter with an open mind and a spirit of adventure.
- Respect the military facility's perimeter and personal space.

11. Nearby Landmarks

- Check out neighboring attractions like the hot springs, ghost villages, and stunning desert vistas.

Curiosity, mystery, and the opportunity to immerse oneself in the history of alien secrets are all offered by visiting Area 51. The trek to this mysterious location is an experience unlike any other, whether you are a fervent believer or a cynic.

Experience The Grand Canyon's Magnificence

Travelers are drawn to the Grand Canyon by its vast grandeur and geological wonders, one of the most breathtaking natural wonders in the world. How to experience the Grand Canyon's magnificence is as follows:

1. The South Rim

- Start your tour at the South Rim, the area of the canyon that is easiest to reach and most commonly traveled.
- Be in awe of the stunning views from vantage points like Yavapai Observation Station and Mather Point.

2. Inn at Grand Canyon

- Tour Grand Canyon Village, the South Rim's storied center.
- For a flavor of the past, stop at the El Tovar Hotel, Kolb Studio, and the Grand Canyon Railway Depot.

3. Hiking Excursions

- Go for a walk on one of the several paths that go down into the canyon.
- Popular choices with differing degrees of difficulty include the Bright Angel Trail and the South Kaibab Trail.

4. Watchtower at Desert View

- To get to Desert View Watchtower, go along the South Rim to the east.
- Explore the tower's Native American-inspired architecture and climb it for panoramic views.

5. Sunup and Sundown

- Take advantage of the opportunity to see the dawn and sunset above the canyon.
- Take the park shuttle as soon as possible to claim a perfect location for dawn, or remain late to see the canyon glow at dusk.

6. Aircraft Tours

- To see the Grand Canyon from an uncommon vantage point, think about taking a helicopter tour.
- Fly over the canyon to get a bird's-eye view of its size and depth.

7. The North Rim

- The North Rim (seasonal access) is a good choice for a more tranquil trip.
- Take in more peace and a little different view of the canyon.

8. Rafting in Whitewater

- For those looking for excitement, consider going whitewater rafting on the Colorado River.
- Travel into the canyon's interior while negotiating exhilarating rapids.

9. Skywalk at the Grand Canyon

- Visit the Grand Canyon Skywalk, a glass-bottomed platform hung above the canyon's brink, on the West Rim.

10. Programs for Rangers

- Participate in ranger-led events and lectures to learn more about the Grand Canyon's geology, history, and ecology.

11. Wilderness Camping

- Reserve permits for backcountry camping and spend the night under the stars for a more memorable experience.

12. Photography

- Use your camera to capture the splendor of the canyon, particularly at dawn and twilight, when the light is most beautiful.

13. Train to the Grand Canyon

- Travel back in time on the Grand Canyon Railway as it runs between Williams and the South Rim.

14. National Park Service

- Attend educational events hosted by the Grand Canyon Conservancy to support the preservation of the Grand Canyon.

15. Make No Trace

- To guarantee that the canyon is preserved for future generations, respect the environment and adhere to the Leave No Trace philosophy.

The Grand Canyon is awe-inspiring and makes for an unforgettable trip. Its enormous size, striking hues, and fascinating history make it a must-visit location for outdoor lovers, hikers, and anybody seeking awe-inspiring natural beauty.

Explore Death Valley's Distinctive Landscape

Death Valley, which lies in both California and Nevada and is recognized for both its harsh desert climate and breathtaking natural beauty, is a place of extremes and contrasts. Here's how to take in Death Valley's distinctive scenery:

1. Visitor Center for Furnace Creek

- Begin your tour at the Furnace Creek Visitor Center, where park rangers may provide you with information, maps, and guidance.

2. Basin of Badwater

- Travel to Badwater Basin to see the enormous salt flats there, which is North America's lowest point.
- Explore the salt crust and be amazed by the fantastical surroundings.

3. A Painter's Palette

- Discover the Artist's Palette in the Black Mountains, a striking geological feature.
- The slopes exhibit a beautiful variety of colors brought forth by different mineral formations.

4. Using Zabriskie Point

- Take a hike to Zabriskie Point for sweeping views of the strikingly formed and worn sedimentary rocks known as the Badlands.

5. Dante's Opinion

- To get a beautiful view of the valley, drive up to Dante's View.

- From this vantage point, you can see the Panamint Range and the enormous salt flats below in all their splendor.

6. Dunes of Mesquite Flat Sand

- Explore Mesquite Flat Sand Dunes, which are close to Stovepipe Wells.

- These dunes are ideal for a peaceful stroll on the smooth sand at dawn or dusk.

7. Grassy Canyon

- Take a hike into Golden Canyon, a confined canyon with mineral-stained, vibrant walls.

- The route links to the Gower Gulch Loop or goes to the Red Cathedral.

8. Observatory Peak

- If you like trekking and have the necessary equipment, climb Telescope Peak, the Panamint Range's highest peak.
- The top offers breathtaking views.

9. Work of Harmony Borax

- Investigate the Harmony Borax Works ruins, a reminder of the region's mining past.
- Get to know the 20-mule teams that previously rode from Death Valley with borax.

10. Golf at Devil's Course

- Take in Devil's Golf Course's unearthly setting, where salt deposits have left the ground with a jagged, pitted surface.

11. Playa Racetrack

- Travel to Racetrack Playa, known for its enigmatic "sailing stones."
- These stones seem to be moving on their own as they leave extensive pathways in the dried mud.

12. Crater of Ubehebe

- Go to the large volcanic crater Ubehebe Crater, which was created by a steam explosion.
- Walk around the crater's rim or enter it from below.

13. Stargazing

- Take in Death Valley's breathtaking nighttime vistas, which are renowned for having little light pollution.
- Participate in ranger-led stargazing events or just relax and take in the cosmic show.

14. Castle Scotty (Closed)

- Although Scotty's Castle is presently closed due to flood damage, it's interesting to explore and is worth keeping an eye on in case it reopens.

15. Safety Measures

- Be ready for erratic weather, particularly during the summer. Carry plenty of supplies and water.

- To protect this sensitive ecology, respect the environment and stick to established pathways.

For those looking for adventure in a rough desert setting, Death Valley is a spectacular location because of its bare beauty, geological marvels, and distinctive natural events. Death Valley provides a memorable experience, whether you're exploring its salt flats, vibrant canyons, or stargazing beneath its starry sky.

Printed in Great Britain
by Amazon

31853869R00106